P9-CQO-322

MARK ECKEL

Timeless Truth

Student Worktext

An Apologetic for the
Reliability,
Authenticity, and
Authority
of the
Bible

MARK
ECKEL

Timeless
Truth

Student Worktext

To enable Christian educators and schools worldwide to effectively pre-
pare students for life

Publishing is a function of the Academic Affairs Department of ACSI. As an organization, ACSI is committed to the ministry of Christian school education, to enable Christian educators and schools worldwide to effectively prepare students for life. As a publisher of books, textbooks, and other resources, ACSI endeavors to produce biblically sound materials that reflect Christian scholarship and stewardship, and that address the identified needs of Christian schools around the world.

For additional information, write ACSI, Academic Affairs Department, PO Box 35097, Colorado Springs, CO 80935-3509.

Printed in the United States of America

Timeless Truth: An Apologetic for the Reliability, Authenticity, and Authority of the Bible - Student

ISBN 1-58331-130-0 Catalog # 7064

Association of Christian Schools International

PO Box 35097 Colorado Springs, CO 80935-3509

Customer Service: 800/367-0798 Website: http://www.acsi.org

About the Author

Mark Eckel is assistant professor of education at Moody Bible Institute. Mark has served as an instructor of his self-developed curriculum *Christian Life and World Studies* (CLAWS), department head, and chaplain in Christian schools for sixteen years. Mark and his wife Robin, with their children Tyler and Chelsea, live in Wheaton, Illinois. Part of Mark's curriculum *Let God Be God*, a semester course for Christian high schools, was published by ACSI in 1997. Mark's self-published book *Biblical Integration: Understanding the World Through the Word* includes hundreds of scriptural principles of integration for immediate classroom use by Christian school teachers. Mark has taught seminars around the country on worldview, culture, apologetics, education, curriculum development, and philosophy. Mark is an ordained minister; he holds a Th.Min. in Old Testament and has begun work on a Ph.D.

105634

v

Interacts

Sergeant Summers was a hero. He single-handedly attacked multiple German-held buildings on June 4, 1944, or D-Day. Eyewitness accounts of his five-hour assault put enemy fatalities at a hundred or more. For his superhuman accomplishments, Summers was awarded a battlefield commission and a Distinguished Service Cross. Those who saw the sergeant's heroics attempted to have the Medal of Honor conferred on him posthumously. But according to Stephen Ambrose in *The Victors: Eisenhower and His Boys: The Men of World War II*, "His story has too much John Wayne/Hollywood in it to be believed, except that more than ten men saw and reported his exploits."

It struck me as I read about Sergeant Summers that the credibility of eyewitnesses can be challenged, as even in our own century some have claimed such evidence to be "unbelievable." The connection to Scripture is obvious. Eyewitness accounts provide a vital framework for the truthfulness of the Gospel message. The reliability of God's Word hinges on the person and work of Jesus, recorded by humans, superintended by the Holy Spirit. If their accounts are wrong, the Christian worldview is susceptible to attack.

And so, for years my students have heard me say this: "I don't want you to believe anything I teach you!" Acts 17:11 is clear: "Now the Bereans were of more noble character than the Thessalonians, for they received the message with great eagerness and examined the Scriptures every day to see if what Paul said was true." Three important ideas stand out: (1) the Bereans studied the Bible individually, (2) they believed it was trustworthy, and (3) they examined it closely to substantiate the claims of a Bible teacher. In order for you to personally own your biblical beliefs, you must be assured of Scripture's reliability. May you, like the Bereans, base your beliefs on your interaction first with the text of Scripture, then with the teacher. May you be convinced of, and rely upon, the veracity of both testaments, their supernatural origin, and their application to everyday life.

Mark Eckel
Wheaton, Illinois
January 2001

Interacts

>Individual Truth Claims:
Truth Is What You Make It

Below are some common assertions about truth. Analyze each statement to understand its assumptions and whether or not it has practical value in real-world situations.

Truth Claims

"There are many truths."

"Truth is what you make it."

"Truth is moral and requires a commitment to a moral life defined by honesty, fairness, courage, and respect for others."

"Truth is determined through knowledge, reason, life experiences, and common sense."

"What is true today may not be true tomorrow."

"What is true for me may not be true for you."

"I know in my heart it's true."

"I cannot impose my truth on another or say that someone's truth is wrong."

"Truth is harmony with nature."

Truth Critiques

Name

>Worldview Truth Claims:
Answering the Big Questions

A worldview is _____
_____
_____
_____

Test the strengths and weaknesses of the following systems of thought as they might be practiced in real-world situations.

(1) Naturalism (secular humanism, atheism, individualism)
A person finds truth in the external world through the five senses and the scientific method.

Strengths _____
_____

Weaknesses _____
_____

(2) Pantheism (Eastern mysticism, Native American religion, New Age beliefs)
The personal experience of becoming one with the universe creates truth that cannot be measured or defined.

_____

Strengths _____
_____

Weaknesses _____
_____

(3) Animism (polytheistic and spiritualist religions)
Truth comes through a witch doctor, shaman, or spirit guide, who interprets dreams and visions to explain what the spirits think and what they want people to do.

_____

Strengths _____
_____

Weaknesses _____
_____

Name

>Worldview Truth Claims: Answering the Big Questions

④ Postmodernism (deconstructionism and multiculturalism)
Truth is relative to the culture or the group: all reality, knowledge, experience, language, history, and ethics are created by those who hold them. All truth claims are to be tolerated.

Strengths _____
_____
_____

Weaknesses _____
_____
_____
_____

⑤ Nihilism
Truth is dead; there is no meaning; nothing matters.

Strengths _____
_____
_____

Weaknesses _____
_____
_____

⑥ Theism (Christianity, Judaism, and Islam)
Truth comes from God through natural and supernatural revelation. Communication from God interprets reality, establishes ethics, and identifies an afterlife.

Strengths _____
_____
_____

Weaknesses _____
_____

>Outside the Lines, No Need to Erase

Read the following verses, and write the statements that describe God as transcendent (outside of and separate from the natural world) and immutable (never changing).

Numbers 23:19, 20 _____

1 Samuel 15:29 _____

Job 11:7–8 _____

Job 26:14 _____

Job 36:26 _____

Job 37:5 _____

Psalm 110:4 _____

Name

Isaiah 44:6

Isaiah 48:12

Isaiah 46:9–11

Malachi 3:6

Romans 2:11

1 Timothy 6:15–16

James 1:17

1. Is either emotion or experience a valid test for truth? Why or why not?

_____

_____

_____

2. How would you respond to the following statements in relation to truth?

"You're asking how you can know he really loves you? Just trust your feelings."

_____

_____

"Hearts don't think; they feel."

_____

_____

"You ask me how I know He lives. He lives within my heart."

_____

_____

_____

3. Do people base their ethics (what they should do) on experience?

_____

_____

_____

4. Does experience have any value? If so, what?

_____

_____

_____

Name

5 Read John 6:1–5. Now read Jesus' comment on the crowd's belief in 6:26. In what were the people most interested? How did their belief differ from that of the disciples in 6:68, 69?

_____

_____

_____

6 Read John 20:24–31. Did Thomas have to experience Jesus' physical resurrection for the resurrection to be true? Why or why not?

_____

_____

_____

7 Read Acts 26. What arguments did Paul use for the validity of Christianity?

_____

_____

_____

_____

8 Evaluate the following statements biblically by reading Proverbs 4 (especially verses 1–4 and 20–23):

a. "Live and learn."

_____

_____

_____

b. "You can't know what I'm going through until you've experienced it yourself."

_____

_____

_____

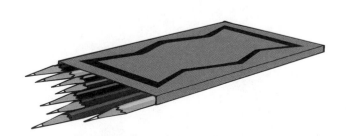

9 If personal experience is a poor foundation for belief, what about the supernatural work of the Holy Spirit in the world? What do these Scriptures teach?

Exodus 31:3–5

2 Samuel 23:2

Psalm 139:7, 23–24

John 16:8–11

Romans 8:9, 16

1 Corinthians 2:10–11

1 Corinthians 2:14

2 Timothy 1:13, 14

Christians must not dismiss, negate, or downplay the work of the Spirit in the world, but they must also know how to substantiate their worldview objectively.

Christianity is reasonable, but it is also beyond reason.

>You Gotta Have Faith!

1 Compare and contrast the following statements. Why does the difference matter?

"I have faith, so my beliefs are true."

_____

_____

"My beliefs are true, so I have faith."

_____

_____

_____

2 Consider what faith isn't.
What do people mean by the following often-heard comments about faith? Is the idea behind each statement biblical, or Christian?

a "You gotta have faith!"

_____

_____

_____

_____

b "Take a leap of faith!"

_____

_____

_____

_____

c "Have faith, and all your problems will end."

_____

_____

_____

_____

Name

>You Gotta Have Faith!

3 Consider what faith is.

▶ **a** Reasonable _____ : this is what I_____ , my _____

Read Hebrews 11:1–3. What important word is repeated five times?_____
Next, complete these sentences. You might want to memorize them too.

Faith is the _____ of things hoped for, the _____
of things not seen. . . .

By faith we _____ that the worlds were framed by the word of God. . . .

Believing something makes it true.   True or False

Truth may lead to belief.   True or False

Read 1 Timothy 4:6. What is biblical faith based on?

_____

_____

▶ **b** Intellectual _____ : this is what I _____

my _____

What two words in Hebrews 11:1 suggest that faith is reliable?

_____

Is it possible to have weak faith? Is it OK to doubt?

_____

_____

_____

_____

_____

_____

_____

>You Gotta Have Faith!

Read James 2:19–20. Can a person know but not have believing faith?

_____

_____

_____

_____

C ▶ Faith leads to personal _____ ; this is what I _____

My _____

What phrase is repeated in Hebrews 11:3, 4, 5, 7, 8, 9, 11, and more?

_____

Why did the writer repeat this phrase as he told about each "hero of faith"?

_____

_____

_____

_____

How do I know that others have faith?

_____

_____

_____

What should faith produce in me?

_____

_____

_____

Name

>The Bible: Why Does It Matter?

1 How do we know anything?

_____

_____

_____

_____

What are my beliefs based on?

_____

_____

_____

_____

_____

_____

_____

2 What would happen to my beliefs if I found out that the Bible is wrong, in whole or in part?

_____

_____

_____

_____

_____

_____

3 Conclusion:

When you question a document's _____ you begin to question its

_____ and ultimately its _____ .

Name

>Ancient Forgeries or Reliable Histories?

1 Did the Bible come from oral tradition (word-of-mouth) or written records?

The Problem

_____

_____

_____

_____

_____

The Solution

▶ **a**
_____

_____

_____

▶ **b**
_____

_____

_____

▶ **c**
_____

_____

_____

2 Are the reproductions of Scripture (the copying or transmission process used by the scribes) reliable? Why is this important?

The Process

_____

_____

_____

_____

_____

Name

The Importance of the Dead Sea Scrolls

A Comparison

_____

_____

_____

	Written	Copy	Time	Extant Copies
The Iliad	c. 900 B.C.	c. 400 B.C.	500 years	643
The NT	c. A.D. 40–90	c. A.D. 125	35–85 years	15,000+

An Illustration:

1400 B.C.	400 B.C.	200 B.C.	A.D. 1000	A.D. 1947
Moses writes	Last OT Book Written	Dead Sea Scrolls Written	Oldest Known Manuscript Prior to DSS	Dead Sea Scrolls Discovered

 3 How do we know these words we have in the twenty-first century are the words of the original first-century writers? Does it matter? Why or why not?

The Solution

_____

_____

_____

_____

_____

_____

>Putting the Paper to Bed: News Stories and the Bible

Answer the following questions. Then compare your ideas with the teacher's.

1 Define and discuss the word *bias*.

Do reporters ever show any prejudice or partiality about the events they report? Does bias ever show in how they write for the newspaper, or what they say on television? How can you tell? Can you give examples?

_____

_____

_____

_____

_____

_____

_____

_____

_____

Did Bible writers have a bias? What examples can you give? How were Bible writers the same as, or different from, today's news reporters?

_____

_____

_____

_____

_____

_____

_____

_____

_____

_____

Name

>Putting the Paper to Bed: News Stories and the Bible

2 In covering an event, how does a reporter discover the facts? How do people go about finding out what happened?

Do you think this was the process used in writing the four Gospels?

3 Can the Bible's sources be trusted? Would the evidence in the Gospel accounts be stronger if there were only one Gospel writer, not four?

What has happened since the Bible was written that might cause some to believe the biblical accounts?

4 Can eyewitnesses be trusted? Why or why not?

_____

_____

_____

_____

_____

How do eyewitnesses help or hinder the credibility of the resurrection?

_____

_____

_____

_____

_____

_____

Would a person be likely to die for something he knew was untrue?

_____

_____

Why not use enemy eyewitnesses to prove something false?

_____

_____

Why not ask them yourself?

_____

_____

Name

>Putting the Paper to Bed: News Stories and the Bible

Why not "pad" or "tweak" the evidence?

_____

_____

_____

_____

_____

_____

_____

Suppose an entertainment columnist, a sports commentator, and a CBS *Evening News* anchorperson all report the same event. How might their stories differ? Are the differences significant? Why or why not?

_____

_____

_____

_____

_____

_____

_____

When we, the audience, finally see or read the stories, what has happened to the information that was gathered in preparation, during the prewriting process?

_____

_____

_____

_____

_____

_____

_____

_____

>What Would You Do If...?

Imagine each situation below, and tell what you think you would do. Be honest. Then read your answers and consider what they tell you about yourself:

What would you do if . . .

1. you had an opportunity to practice what you're best at?

_____

2. you were a famous scientist, and you could cure just one disease?

_____

3. you were the chief officer of the United Nations?

_____

4. you could go anywhere and do anything in the world?

_____

5. you could spend time talking with any person, living or dead?

_____

6. you had just twenty-four hours to live?

_____

7. your house was burning, and you could save only one possession?

_____

8. you could eliminate one day from the history of the world?

_____

9. you had to give up four of your five senses?

_____

10. you could give anything you chose to a needy person?

_____

Name _____

>What's Most Important?

Read each Scripture and answer this question: What truth about God's Word does the passage present?

1 Luke 8:4–18 Use it or lose it.

_____

_____

_____

_____

_____

2 Luke 16:19–31 Ignore God's Word in this life, and be ignored by the God of the Word in the next life.

_____

_____

_____

_____

_____

3 Luke 24:13–49 To know God, one must know His Word.

_____

_____

_____

_____

_____

4 Conclusion

_____

_____

_____

_____

_____

Name

>Show Me What Ya' Got!
A Truth Workout

1 Skim 1 and 2 Timothy and Titus. Jot down the reference for each occurrence of the words *truth*, *true*, and *the truth*. Consider the context, and the fact that these letters were written to young pastors. *Why did Paul emphasize truth? What does* the truth *refer to?*

_____

_____

_____

_____

2 *Should we seek for, or inquire about, truth? Is it wrong to seek, or to question? What is something in the Christian worldview that you have doubted is true? Have you ever resolved the issue? Why or why not? What can happen if truth issues are left unresolved or unanswered?* Write down a key phrase or sentence from each verse or passage below to help answer these questions.

Proverbs 23:23

_____

_____

Proverbs 25:2

_____

_____

2 Timothy 2:14–19

_____

_____

_____

2 Thessalonians 2:9–12

_____

_____

2 Thessalonians 2:13–15

_____

_____

Name

>Show Me What Ya' Got!
A Truth Workout

3 Do others see the truth in us? Write down the character qualities, or traits, that reflect truthfulness in the lives of the people mentioned in these verses.

Exodus 18:21 _____

2 Chronicles 19:9 _____

Nehemiah 7:2 _____

Nehemiah 9:8 _____

Proverbs 12:22 _____

Proverbs 13:17 _____

Proverbs 14:5 _____

Proverbs 14:22 _____

1Corinthians 4:2 _____

2 Corinthians 3:2 _____

Ephesians 4:15 _____

Ephesians 4:25 _____

Philippians 4:3 _____

Philippians 4:8 _____

Titus 2:7 _____

Titus 2:10 _____

2 John 4 _____

3 John 3, 4 _____

3 John 12 _____

>Word of Mouth or Word of Pen?

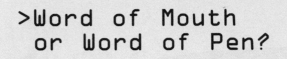

1 Each verse or passage below reveals something about how God communicates with humans. Write key words from each verse about God's method of communication.

Exodus 34:27

Deuteronomy 17:18–20

Deuteronomy 31:9

Deuteronomy 31:22–26

Joshua 24:25, 26

1 Samuel 10:25

2 Chronicles 21:12–15

Name

>Word of Mouth
or Word of Pen?

Isaiah 30:8 _____
_____
_____

Isaiah 34:16 _____
_____
_____

Jeremiah 8:8 _____
_____
_____

Jeremiah 29:1 _____
_____
_____

Jeremiah 30:2 _____
_____
_____

Jeremiah 36:4 _____
_____
_____

Hosea 8:12 _____
_____
_____

2 What conclusion can you draw about what should be important to us as believers?

_____
_____
_____

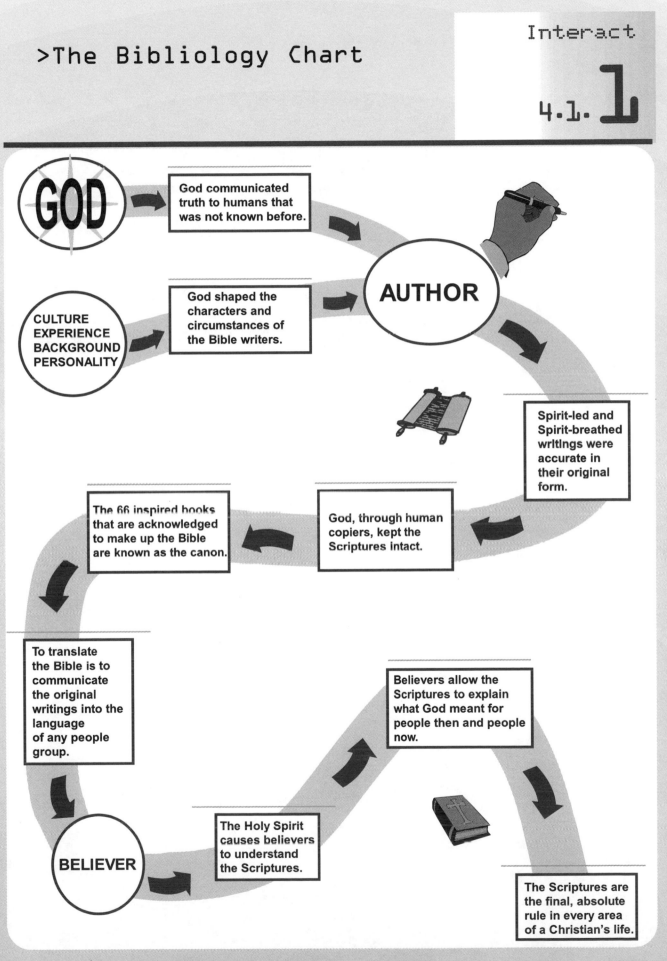

GOD

God communicated truth to humans that was not known before.

AUTHOR

CULTURE
EXPERIENCE
BACKGROUND
PERSONALITY

God shaped the characters and circumstances of the Bible writers.

Spirit-led and Spirit-breathed writings were accurate in their original form.

The 66 inspired books that are acknowledged to make up the Bible are known as the canon.

God, through human copiers, kept the Scriptures intact.

To translate the Bible is to communicate the original writings into the language of any people group.

Believers allow the Scriptures to explain what God meant for people then and people now.

BELIEVER

The Holy Spirit causes believers to understand the Scriptures.

The Scriptures are the final, absolute rule in every area of a Christian's life.

Name

1 Where did the following words originate?

Bible and *paper*

_____

_____

_____

_____

_____

Old and New Testaments

_____

_____

_____

_____

_____

2 Read Hebrews 1:1–2. In what two ways had God spoken to His people in the past, and how do they correspond to the main parts of the Bible?

_____

_____

3 Look up and read the following verses, and answer the questions below:

Matthew 21:42; 22:29   Acts 8:32

Mark 12:10   Romans 1:2

Luke 24:32   Galatians 3:22

John 5:39   2 Timothy 3:15, 16

What is the repeated phrase in these verses? _____

For believer in New Testament times, what did the phrase refer to? _____

>You Can't Judge a Book by Its Cover!

BIBLE MATH FACTS	*The Old Testament is 77% of the Bible. *97% of the New Testament is from the OT. *Only 3% of the NT is unique information.

So why study the Old Testament?

_____

_____

Why did God continue to communicate with humans in the New Testament?

_____

_____

Who is the connecting link between the Old and New Testaments?

_____

_____

THINKING QUESTION Read Ezekiel 2:9–3:3

God is speaking metaphorically; by "eating" He means to take it in, understand it, allow its "nourishment" to sustain the reader. As Jeremiah says, "I found your words, ate them, and they were the joy and delight of my heart."

(Hint: Read Ezekiel 1:1 and 3:4 with Jeremiah 15:16.)

What does this mean for me today?
Apply the "internalization" principle of Scripture.
How should we "take in" God's Word?

>A Bird's-Eye-View of the Scriptures

The Bible can be summarized in three words:

1.
2.
3.

The Bible can be summarized in a picture:

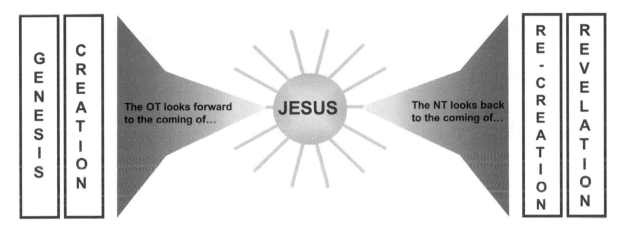

G E N E S I S

C R E A T I O N

The OT looks forward to the coming of...

JESUS

The NT looks back to the coming of...

RE - C R E A T I O N

R E V E L A T I O N

The Bible overviews God's plan for all people:

God works with . . .

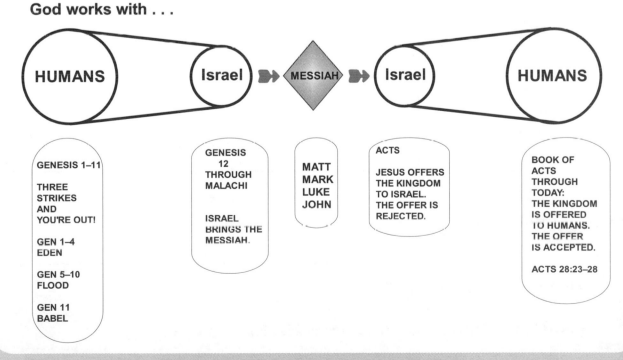

HUMANS

Israel

MESSIAH

Israel

HUMANS

GENESIS 1–11

THREE STRIKES AND YOU'RE OUT!

GEN 1–4 EDEN

GEN 5–10 FLOOD

GEN 11 BABEL

GENESIS 12 THROUGH MALACHI

ISRAEL BRINGS THE MESSIAH.

MATT MARK LUKE JOHN

ACTS

JESUS OFFERS THE KINGDOM TO ISRAEL. THE OFFER IS REJECTED.

BOOK OF ACTS THROUGH TODAY: THE KINGDOM IS OFFERED TO HUMANS. THE OFFER IS ACCEPTED.

ACTS 28:23–28

Name

>A Bird's-Eye-View
of the Scriptures

THE BIBLE WAS WRITTEN . . .

over **TIME**		
in **LANGUAGES**		
on **CONTINENTS**		
by **AUTHORS**		
as **LITERATURE**		
about **REAL PEOPLE**		
among **CULTURES**		

WHO TIES IT ALL TOGETHER? _____

(Read Luke 24:13–27, especially verses 25–27.)

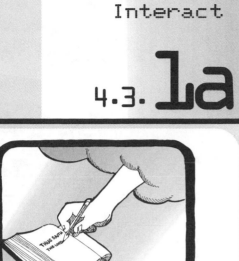

"Revelation" means . . .

_____

_____

Why is it important that God communicate with humans?

_____

_____

People need a source of...

TRUTH either _____ or _____

FAITH either _____ or _____

Make a list of forms of communication that are used today:

_____

_____

Now list all the ways God has given messages to people:

_____

_____

Name

>Revelation

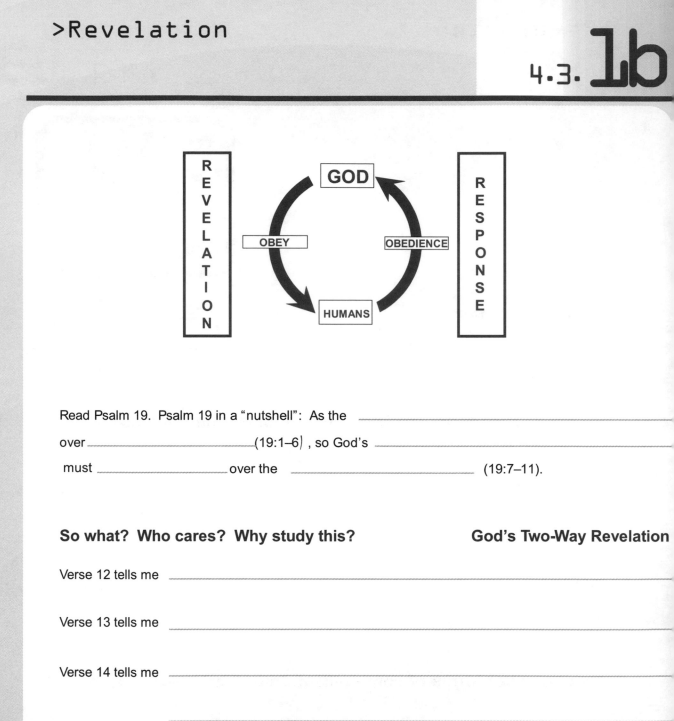

Read Psalm 19. Psalm 19 in a "nutshell": As the _____

over _____ (19:1–6) , so God's _____

must _____ over the _____ (19:7–11).

So what? Who cares? Why study this?   **God's Two-Way Revelation**

Verse 12 tells me _____

Verse 13 tells me _____

Verse 14 tells me _____

_____

The Bible was written over 2,000 years ago. How can it speak to the issues of the 21st century?

What are the assumptions?

_____

_____

_____

_____

_____

What are the answers?

_____

_____

_____

_____

_____

_____

_____

_____

CONCLUSION

_____

_____

_____

Name

Christianity has failed. The gospel has not altered the awful state of the world. The Bible is outdated.

What is the assumption?

_____

_____

What is the answer?

_____

_____

_____

_____

_____

_____

CONCLUSION

_____

_____

Christians use circular reasoning. They say the Bible is inspired because Jesus said so. Then they conclude Jesus is God because inspired Scripture says so.

What is the assumption?

_____

_____

What is the answer?

_____

_____

_____

_____

_____

Name _____

```
( The Gospels     )  →  ( The Gospels      )  →  ( Jesus says     )
( are historical  )     ( tell of Jesus    )     ( Scripture Is   )
( documents.      )     ( as Lord.         )     ( inspired.      )
```

>Preparation of Bible Writers

List all the writers of Scripture you can think of:

_____

_____

_____

The Bible is at the same time

_____

_____

_____

Preparation means that

_____

_____

_____

Preparation examples: Jeremiah 1:4, 5; Galatians 1:14–16

Both writers were prepared from

_____

_____

_____

Draw the action in Acts 27:15. As God moved the writers, they could still move freely in the boat.

Always remember

_____

_____

_____

The Bible writers were neither _____ nor _____

If they had been, all Scripture would have been the same in its format, style, and vocabulary. Compare Moses' law code in Exodus 20 with Paul's statement about law in 1 Timothy 1:8–11.

Name

46

>Some Bible Writers You Know

Now take a closer look. Find and read the Scripture about each writer named below. Record information about how each was prepared to write the book(s) he wrote.

1 **Moses** Acts 7:20–22; Hebrews 11:23–28

_____

_____

_____

_____

_____

2 **Solomon** 1 Kings 4:29–34

_____

_____

_____

_____

3 **Luke** Colossians 4:14; Luke 4:1–4; Acts 1:1–3

_____

_____

_____

_____

4 **Paul** Acts 8:1–4; 22:1–5; 26:4–11; Galatians 1:14–16; Philippians 3:1–6

_____

_____

_____

_____

Name

>Changing Time Zones

1 Read the prediction and its fulfilment in Scripture. Write the fulfillment.

a Compare Micah 5:2 with Matthew 2:1 and Luke 2:1–7.

Prediction: (700 B.C.) The Messiah's birthplace will be Bethlehem.

Fulfillment: (4 B.C.) _____

b Compare Isaiah 7:14 with Matthew 1:18–25.

Prediction: (730 B.C.) A virgin will bear a son.

Fulfillment: (4 B.C.) _____

c Compare Isaiah 53:7 with Matthew 27:12–14.

Prediction: (715 B.C.) At His trial the Messiah would be silent before His accusers.

Fulfillment: (A.D. 29) _____

d Compare Psalm 22:14–18 with Luke 23:27, 34, 35 and John 19:29 and 20:25.

Prediction: (700 B.C.)   Details of the Messiah's death are described.

Fulfillment: (A.D. 29zf) _____

_____

2 You have seen above how prophecies given hundreds of years earlier were fulfilled in Jesus. Why are these fulfilled prophecies significant for unbelievers? for believers?

_____
_____
_____
_____
_____
_____
_____
_____

3 Read each passage listed below. Summarize each prediction and its fulfillment.

Prediction	Fulfillment
a. Genesis 49:10	Matthew 1:2; Luke 3:23, 33
b. Psalm 2:6	Matthew 21:5; 27:37
c. Psalm 16:10	Acts 2:31
d. Psalm 110:4	Hebrews 5:5, 6
e. Psalm 118:22	Romans 9:32, 33; 1 Peter 2:7
f. Isaiah 11:1	Matthew 1:6; Luke 3:23, 32

Prediction	Fulfillment
g. Isaiah 50:6	Matthew 26:67
h. Isaiah 53:5	Matthew 27:26
i. Isaiah 61:1, 2	Luke 4:16–21
j. Jeremiah 23:5	Matthew 1:1
k. Jeremiah 31:15	Matthew 2:16
l. Zechariah 9:9	Matthew 21:6–11
m. Zechariah 11:12–13	Matthew 27:3–7

Name

>The Inspiration of Scripture

(1) Why is revelation not enough?

_____

_____

(2) The inspiration of Scripture means that

_____

_____

(3) The inspiration equation:

_____ **+** _____ **=**

(4) What the inspiration of Scripture is *not:*

_____

_____

_____

_____

_____

_____

_____

(5) What inspiration *is:* read 2 Timothy 3:16.

In English: _____

In Greek: _____

_____

(6) How did the inspiration of Scripture happen? 2 Peter 1:20, 21 (see the picture above). Did the prophets make up what they wrote?

_____

_____

Were the writers or the writings inspired?

_____

_____

Name

>The Inspiration of Scripture

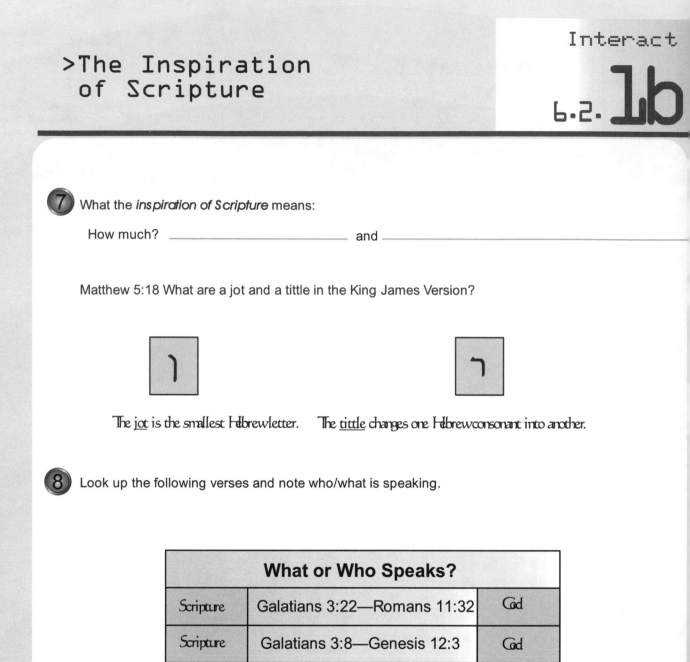

7 What the *inspiration of Scripture* means:

How much? _____ and _____

Matthew 5:18 What are a jot and a tittle in the King James Version?

The <u>jot</u> is the smallest Hebrew letter.   The <u>tittle</u> changes one Hebrew consonant into another.

8 Look up the following verses and note who/what is speaking.

	What or Who Speaks?	
Scripture	Galatians 3:22—Romans 11:32	God
Scripture	Galatians 3:8—Genesis 12:3	God
Scripture	Romans 9:17—Exodus 9:16	God

What conclusion can you draw from this correlation?

_____

_____

_____

_____

9 Write brief answers to the following thought questions on the inspiration of Scripture:

a Since God inspired the words of the Bible, what words can you use to describe it?

_____

_____

b If the Bible were only humanly inspired, what would be the implications for my faith?

_____

_____

c If the Bible is only inspired "when it speaks to me," what would be true about its authority?

_____

_____

d What is wrong with human authority saying, "Because I said so!"?

_____

_____

10 What problems arise if God inspired only the thoughts, but not the words, of Scripture?

_____

_____

11 Using a Bible dictionary, concordance, or word book, discuss and apply the following words from 2 Timothy 3:16, 17.

a useful: _____

_____

b teaching: _____

_____

c rebuking: _____

_____

d correcting: _____

_____

e training: _____

_____

f thoroughly equipped: _____

_____

1 Use a dictionary to do a study of the etymology (origin) of the following words to discover their root meanings.

a doctrine _____

b orthodoxy _____

c catechism _____

d creed _____

Why are these words crucial for the Christian? Why are extrabiblical words at times useful to delineate or elaborate on a point of teaching?

_____

2 According to the Bible, how important is doctrine, and why?

a Acts 2:42 _____

b Romans 16:17–19 _____

c Ephesians 4:11–16 _____

d Colossians 2:6–8 _____

e 2 Thessalonians 2:15 _____

f 1 Timothy 4:11–16 _____

g Titus 1:9–14 _____

Name

(3) People tend to gloss over the importance of ideas, thoughts, or teachings while putting more emphasis on deeds. Should they? Why or why not?

_____

_____

_____

_____

(4) Bring to class two doctrinal statements, perhaps your church's and your school's. Discuss similarities and differences. Why are points of doctrine the same for most or all Christians?

_____

_____

_____

_____

(5) Is it important to pass these basic beliefs to the next generation (2 Timothy 2:2)? Why?

_____

_____

_____

_____

>Heresy in the Church

1) Do a study of the etymology (origin) of the words *heresy* and *tradition*.

_____

_____

_____

_____

_____

_____

_____

2) Read the following passages taking note of statements warning of heresy and the church's response to it.

Acts 15:1 _____

_____

_____

Acts 20:25–31 _____

_____

_____

Romans 16:17–19 _____

_____

_____

Ephesians 4:14 _____

_____

Colossians 2:16–22 _____

_____

_____

Name

1 Timothy 4:1, 2 _____

1 Timothy 6:3–5 _____

2 Timothy 2:14–26 _____

2 Timothy 4:3 _____

Titus 1:9–14 _____

Hebrews 13:9 _____

2 Peter 2:1 _____

3 Respond to the following statements:

a Heresy points to truth.

_____

b Truth precedes heresy.

_____

c Better to be a heretic than a skeptic.

_____

d One to whom truth is given is second in importance to the truth itself.

_____

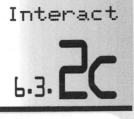

4 When should variant and disputed positions be heard, or defended, or condemned? What is the basis for condemning heresies? What are the positives or negatives of condemning heresies?

_____

_____

_____

_____

_____

_____

Is it possible that differences may sharpen or define a situation? What of the leader who is afraid of losing control (e.g., 3 John)? Can a negative view of a person be used as an *ad hominem* (against the person) attack?

_____

_____

_____

_____

Name

5 What should false teaching in the early church teach us today?

_____

_____

_____

_____

_____

_____

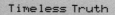

>Jesus' Person and Authority

Look up the following verses, and summarize the important point that each makes concerning Jesus' verbal authority.

John 6:67–69 _____

_____

Luke 3:22 _____

Luke 9:35 _____

_____

John 6:35– 36 _____

_____

John 7:37–38 _____

_____

John 14:6 _____

_____

Matthew 7:28–29 _____

_____

Mark 1:22 _____

_____

Luke 4:32 _____

_____

Matthew 9:6, 8 _____

_____

John 17:6–8 _____

_____

Matthew 5:17 _____

_____

Mark 2:23–28 _____

_____

Matthew 26:24, 54 _____

_____

Luke 24:27 _____

_____

Luke 24:44 _____

_____

John 5:39 _____

Name

Write a brief description of what Jesus validated by His words from the Old Testament. Think about *why* this is important.

Matthew 11:1–6 (see Isaiah 35:5, 6) _____

Matthew 12:3 _____

Matthew 15:3–6 _____

Matthew 19:4–6 _____

Matthew 22:29–32 _____

Matthew 22:37–39 _____

Matthew 22:43–45 _____

Matthew 23:35 _____

_____

Matthew 24:15 _____

Matthew 24:37–38 _____

Mark 7:6 _____

Mark 12:26 _____

Luke 4:25 _____

Luke 17:29, 32 _____

John 3:14 _____

John 6:31–32 _____

John 7:19 _____

John 8:56 _____

John 12:38–41 _____

John 19:28 _____

Name

>Predictions, Prognostications, and Prophecies

Consider each situation described below, and answer the questions that follow.

1 A "spirituality" speaker comes to your town claiming connection to ancient messages. She says to "follow your heart," "listen to your inner voice," "question authority," and that "truth is seldom found in someone else's words; search for it."

a Would you be drawn to a person claiming a "spiritual" connection? Why or why not?

_____

_____

b "Ancient messages" would seem to be something positive and desirable. What further information should you want to know?

_____

_____

c Reflect on each of the statements in quotation marks above. Ask, What does it mean? How does it compare with what the Bible says?

_____

_____

_____

_____

2 A nationally known "seer" has had many predictions come true. People are amazed by his high rate of success in "unveiling the future." According to news reports, many people pay money in the hope of winning at Lotto, picking a winner at the track, or even finding true love.

a What questions would you ask about the person's predictions?

_____

_____

b How high would the success rate have to be to confirm this seer's trustworthiness?

_____

c Why do you think people are so interested in the future?

_____

_____

d Does the request for money pose any problems? If so, what might they be?

_____

_____

Name

3 A local church advertises that a pastor from another part of the country will speak on how to interpret dreams and symbols. It is promised that he will shed "light on your night."

Why doesn't the local pastor have this ability?

_____

_____

_____

What is necessary to interpret dreams and symbols?

_____

_____

_____

How can you know that another's interpretation of your dream is correct?

_____

_____

_____

Some psychologists suggest solutions to questions about the meaning of a dream. What is the difference between the psychologist and the pastor? Suppose they disagree. How can a person know whose interpretation is right?

_____

_____

_____

>Canonization:
What Books Belong
in the Bible?

1 The two essential elements of inspiration are:

_____

_____

_____

2 Canonization means:

_____

_____

_____

_____

3 The word *canon* came from a Greek word meaning:

_____

4 *Canon* came to be known as:

_____

5 So the canon is the _____ the _____ or accepted rule for Christians.

The canon consists of the books officially recognized as:

_____

6 At the Council of Carthage (A.D. 397), the church did not _____ or _____ what books would be in the Bible (the canon). They simply _____ or _____ God's Word.

7 But what qualification marks which writings are from God? _____

8 But how do we know which authors to accept?

a Deuteronomy 13:1–5

_____

_____

b Deuteronomy 18:17–20

_____

_____

_____

_____

c Deuteronomy 18:21–22

_____

_____

_____

_____

d Acts 1:21–22

_____

_____

_____

_____

e Ephesians 1:9–10

_____

_____

_____

>Canonization:
Prophets and Apostles

1 What is the importance of the prophets and apostles in establishing the canon?

a The *prophets were* _____

b Matthew 5:17–19 _____

c Luke 16:16, 17 _____

d Luke16:29–31 _____

e Luke 24:25, 27 _____

f Acts 28:25 _____

g 1 Peter 1:10–12 _____

h Hebrews 1:1, 2 _____

i The *apostles* were _____

j Matthew 19:28 _____

k John 14:26 _____

l John 16:13 _____

m John 17:20 _____

n 1 Corinthians 12:28 _____

o Ephesians 2:20 _____

Name

2 If you don't like to have other people tell you what to believe, canonization is of utmost importance to you. Look up the following passages and record each writer's view of authorship as a test of orthodox

a Galatians 1:6–10 _____

_____

b 2 Corinthians 11:1–4 _____
and 13-15
_____

_____

c Ephesians 4:11–16 _____

d Colossians 2:6–8 _____

e 2 Timothy 2 15–19 _____
and 24–26
_____

3 Make a list of those people, groups, or beliefs in our culture that clearly or subtly tell us what and why to believe.

_____

_____

4 Now discuss, with the Scriptures you read as your base, how Christians can and should defend themselves and counter or refute opposing beliefs.

_____

_____

_____

_____

_____

5 Finally, explain in your own words why canonization is expecially important in our culture today.

_____

_____

_____

>In the Bookshop: How It Fits Together

Sometimes the practical questions cause more confusion than the theological issues. Discuss the questions below with partners or in small groups.

1 How many books did Moses write?

_____

_____

_____

2 Did Moses write the book of Deuteronomy?

_____

3 If Moses wrote Deuteronomy, how could he write about his own death in chapter 34?

_____

4 If Moses didn't write Deuteronomy 34, who did? Is there a problem of authorship here? Why or why not?

_____

_____

5 Read the following Scriptures: 1 Samuel 10:25; 1 Chronicles 25:5; 29:29; 2 Chronicles 9:29; 12:15; 20:34; 26:22; 29:30 and 32:32. Now look up Numbers 11:25. Does the phrase "a succession of prophets" make sense when you think about how the Bible was put together? What potential problems could you foresee in this method? Do the requirements of Deuteronomy 13 and 18 help?

_____

_____

_____

6 Do we know the names of all the prophets who wrote the Old Testament? Read Acts 13:27, Romans 1:2, and 2 Peter 1:19 for clues. Does this question pose a problem for Christians concerning canonization? Why or why not?

_____

_____

_____

_____

Name

7 What do Deuteronomy 31:24–26 and Joshua 24:26 teach about prophets and their writings?

_____

_____

8 Why are the Old Testament books divided the way they are? Compare 2 Chronicles 36:23 and Ezra 1:1–3. How does this likeness solve the problem?

_____

_____

_____

9 What do the following verses say about Bible writers' views of other Bible writers or their writings: 1 Timothy 4:13; 2 Peter 3:15, 16; Jude 17, 18?

_____

_____

_____

_____

_____

10 Did each apostle think his work was inspired? See 1 Corinthians 14:37; 1 Thessalonians 2:13; 2 Thessalonians 3:14–17; 2 Peter 3:2; Revelation 22:18. Why would this be important?

_____

_____

_____

_____

11 Within fifty years after the New Testament was completed, many church fathers, or "apostolic fathers" (disciples of the apostles themselves), quoted the New Testament. What would this say about the New Testament's authority?

_____

_____

_____

_____

>If We Can't Trust the Bible, Then What?

If the inerrant inspiration of the Bible in its original form is suspect, then we impugn:

(1) The witness of _____

What did Jesus believe about the Old Testament?

Matthew 5:17–19 _____

_____

Matthew 12:40 _____

Luke 4:25–26 _____

_____

Luke 17:29–32 _____

_____

John 5:39–40, 46–47 _____

_____

John 10:35 _____

If _____ is in question, _____ is in question.

(2) The witness of _____

Evaluate the accuracy of this statement: The Bible contains the Word of God.

_____

_____

_____

A syllogism   Major Premise: _____

_____

Minor Premise: _____

_____

Conclusion: _____

_____

Any attack on the Bible is _____

Name

>If We Can't Trust the Bible, Then What?

3 The witness of _____

How was the Holy Spirit involved in the writing of Scripture?

2 Samuel 23:2 _____
_____

Mark 12:36 _____
_____

Acts 1:16 _____
_____

1 Peter 1:10, 11 _____
_____

4 The witness of _____ Scripture says Scripture is from God.

"Thus says the LORD" is repeated _____ times in the Old Testament.

Acts 7:38 _____
_____

Romans 3:2 _____
_____

Hebrews 5:12 _____
_____

If Scripture is suspect in one part, _____

5 The witness of Scripture to its own _____

Record the statements the Bible makes about itself:

Psalm 12:6 _____

_____

Psalm 119 _____

_____

_____

Matthew 4:4, 7, 10 _____

_____

_____

Luke 16:27–31 _____

_____

_____

1 Thessalonians 2:13 _____

_____

Read Hosea 4:6 and Mark 12:24; then complete this sentence: Any doctrinal error is caused by lack

of _____

Make a list of human authorities in your life: _____

What would happen if a nation or organization lost its authority?

_____

_____

Read Romans 13:1–7, Ephesians 6:1–3, and 1 Peter 2:13–18. Then answer the following questions: Does it matter how we treat, talk to, or talk about the authorities in our life? Why or why not? Consider the authority of Scripture and the human authorities in your life. How are they related?

_____

_____

Does a person have to earn respect, or should it be given automatically? Consult 1 Thessalonians 5:12, 13 and Hebrews 13:17.

_____

Name

>Preservation of Scripture

1 Preservation of Scripture means that:

_____

_____

2 Are there any errors in my copy of God's Word? Circle *yes* or *no*. But . . .

a ▶ _____

_____

b ▶ _____

_____

c ▶ _____

3 Amazing statistics. The Bible was written: over a period of _____ years

in _____ languages _____

on _____ continents _____

with _____ materials _____

by _____ authors

4 The difference between *inspiration* and *preservation*:

Inspiration: _____

Preservation: _____

_____

_____

Name

>Preservation of Scripture

5 So are the second, third, fourth, and one hundredth copies of Scripture trustworthy? Read each Scripture below and record whether or not believers 2000 *plus* years ago trusted *copies* of Scripture as authoritative.

Deuteronomy 10:2–4 _____

Deuteronomy 17:18–20 _____

Deuteronomy 31:24–28 _____

2 Chronicles 34:29–31 _____

Jeremiah 36:27, 28 _____

Luke 4:16–21 _____

Acts 17:11 _____

6 What difference does all this make? Why is preservation important?

a ▸ _____

b ▸ _____

c ▸ _____

d ▸ _____

e ▸ _____

1 Copy the Bible book or section that your teacher wants you to copy on a piece of your own paper.

2 Trade copies with a partner. Mark the errors your partner made in spelling, grammar, and punctuation. Take back your own paper and do the following:

a Record the number of words in your book or section: _____

b Record the number of grammar errors in your book or section: _____

c Record the number of punctuation errors: _____

d Record the number of spelling errors: _____

3 Examine your paper for completeness.

a Were any words left out? How many? _____

b Were any words changed? How many? _____

c How do these mistakes affect the passage? _____

4 What problems caused the errors you identified (i.e., skipped a line, missed a word, connected a word to a similar word later in the text).

_____

5 What techniques could you have used to increase your accuracy?

_____

6 Using the following formula, calculate the percentage of error in the copy:

$$\frac{\text{number of errors x 100\%}}{\text{number of words + number of punctuation marks}} = \text{percent inaccurate}$$

7 Assume the copy we have today has been copied once every century. Since it was originally written about A.D. 100 and it is now more than 1,900 years later, the document has been recopied at least nineteen times. Multiply your percentage of error by 19 to arrive at the percentage of error a document might contain today.

_____

8 Reflect on what accounts for the high degree of accuracy in Scripture.

_____

Name

>How the Bible
Came to Us

1 The materials that people first wrote the Bible on were?

_____

2 The copies of Scripture were kept in _____

3 The Old Testament was written in the _____ languages.

4 The New Testament was written in _____

5 Common people did not have their own personal copies of Scripture because

_____

6 Why was the New Testament written?

_____

7 The scriptorium was

_____

_____

_____

8 A codex was

_____

9 Codicies (plural of codex) were made from

_____

10 Early translations of the Bible were made in

_____

11 The emperor Constantine ordered

_____

12 In the fourth century, Jerome translated the Bible

_____

13 Jerome's translation was called

_____

Name

14   Monks in monasteries preserved the Scriptures

_____

15   The church gave parts of the Bible to the people through its

_____

16   Why did the people want the Bible in their own language?

_____

17   Why didn't the church want that to happen?

_____

_____

18   The first English Bible was translated by _____

19   His followers, called "the Lollards,"

_____

20   The three major events that changed the way the Bible came to us were

_____

_____

_____

21   The first English Bible printed on a press was written by _____

22   In 1611, the English King James I gave permission to produce

_____

23   The first publisher of Bibles in the United States was _____

24   Groups of people organized to give people God's Word in their own language are called

_____

Take notes during the film, and discuss these questions at the end:

1 What were the social, economic, political, and religious conditions in Wycliffe's world?

_____

2 Wycliffe protested several of the teachings and practices of the medieval church. Name three of these to which he objected. _____

What was the root cause of his objection to all these practices?

_____

3 In what situations did Wycliffe believe the state could exercise authority over the church?

_____

_____

What support for his theory of dominion (or the authority of the church and state) did he find in Scripture?

_____

_____

In your opinion, how valid are his arguments for the right of the state to take over church property?

_____

4 How did Wycliffe believe the church should use its wealth?

_____

5 When Wycliffe and John of Gaunt were discussing transubstantiation, John of Gaunt said, "It is believed throughout the whole of Christendom." Wycliffe replied, "The fact that something is believed by the multitudes does not necessarily make it true." What belief that does not follow Scripture may be held by a majority in the church today?

_____

 6 The authorities tried to weaken Wycliffe's influence by removing him from Oxford. As noted in the film, however, "a great loss can provide great opportunity to reassess one's life, to discover a new direction." How did Wycliffe's influence actually increase after he left Oxford?

_____

_____

_____

7 What were some arguments the church used against putting the Bible in English?

_____

_____

_____

_____

What counterarguments could Wycliffe and his followers use for putting the Bible in English?

_____

_____

_____

_____

_____

_____

8 In what ways was Wycliffe's influence still felt after his death?

_____

_____

_____

_____

_____

9 In John Wycliffe's time, tradition and custom were replacing the Bible's authority. What traditions and customs that we follow today have usurped the Bible's authority? How can we apply the lessons of Wycliffe's life and ministry to our own?

_____

_____

_____

_____

_____

_____

>John Wycliffe Today

1 Read Acts 17:11 and 1 John 2:20–27. Was Wycliffe right in desiring to place the Bible in the hands of every person? Is it right that everyone should have an opportunity to decide for him- or herself what truth really is? Comment on the following statement: "Make no apology for what you believe and make no attempt to get others to believe it."

_____

_____

_____

_____

2 What was the role of the Lollards? Why were they important to Wycliffe's work in placing Scripture in the lives of the people?

_____

_____

_____

_____

3 What role has the Bible played in shaping the thinking of our world? List all that you can think of.

_____

_____

_____

_____

4 Wycliffe was seen as a scholar in Europe. Discuss how God uses brilliant people to help begin brand new periods of thinking throughout history (i.e., Paul, Augustine, Calvin, Luther, Wesley, Edwards, and many others). Is scholarship important to the church? Why or why not? What are some of its dangers and benefits?

_____

_____

_____

_____

Name

5 Wycliffe's life and work was not fully appreciated until many years later. Comment on what it must feel like to die and yet not see your dreams and plans fulfilled. Read Psalm 71:14–18 and 78:1–8. What is the responsibility of one generation to the next? Are you ever frustrated when God's purposes and timetable don't seem to be yours? How do we as Christians reconcile our human plans with those of the Almighty?

_____

_____

_____

_____

_____

6 Wycliffe was a person of privilege and wealth, yet he stood up for the less advantaged. Should rich people abandon their riches or position to identify with the poor? Why or why not? How should those who are poor respond to those who are rich? Read 1 Timothy 6:6–19.

_____

_____

John Milton commented on John Wycliffe in his work entitled *Aeropagitica*. Thoughtfully read his comment:

> For when God shakes a kingdom with strong and healthful commotions to a general reforming, It is not untrue that many sectaries and false teachers are then busiest in seducing; but yet more true it is, that God then raises to His own work men of rare abilities, and more than common industry, not only to look back and revise what hath been taught heretofore, but to gain further and go on some new enlightened steps in the discovery of truth. For such is the order of God's enlightening His church, to dispense and deal out by degrees His beam, so as our earthly eyes may best sustain it.

What did Milton mean, and how should it affect us today?

_____

_____

_____

_____

1 Who were some of the leading men in England with whom Tyndale had to contend?

Why were they opposed to Tyndale's translating the Bible into English?

_____

_____

_____

2 Tyndale and his evangelical cohorts were smuggling the Bible and religious works into England from continental Europe. Wasn't that going against the laws of England? Don't the Scriptures say the Christian is to be obedient to the powers that be? Was Tyndale right in breaking the laws in this way? Support your position from Scripture.

_____

_____

_____

3 What does the house Cardinal Wolsey built for himself tell you about his character and his attitude to his priestly office?

_____

_____

4 Why would teaching children in English be considered such a crime? Do you think any such laws could be passed in today's world?

_____

_____

5 What was the great idea Tyndale conceived while a tutor at Little Sodbury Manor?

_____

What abilities did he have to accomplish this?

_____

6 Why did Tyndale want to work for Cuthbert Tunstall, the Bishop of London?

_____

What objections did Tunstall give for accepting Tyndale's proposal?

_____

_____

7 How did the merchants encourage the cause of reformation in England?

_____

Name

>William Tyndale:
God's Outlaw

8 Even in Europe, Tyndale faced obstacles to preparing a Bible in English for his countrymen. What difficulties did he face?

_____

_____

9 How did the Archbishop of Canterbury unwittingly help Tyndale in his work?

_____

_____

10 After having escaped capture for years, Tyndale was finally arrested by the authorities. How did this come about?

_____

How did you feel about Henry Phillips' treatment of Tyndale?

_____

What did Phillips do just before Tyndale's arrest that revealed the depths of his degraded character?

_____

11 Tyndale was arrested by the agents of the Emperor Charles, not by any authority of the King of England. The accusations brought against Tyndale again show the close association between church and state in that day. What were the accusations?

_____

_____

_____

12 What was Tyndale's belief about the roles of faith and works in the believer's life?

_____

_____

13 What was William Tyndale's dying prayer?

_____

Was it ever answered?

_____

1. William Tyndale was a man of passionate belief. How are ardent supporters of belief or purveyors of a position treated in our day? Why are these people necessary? List positive and negative traits of such folks.

2. What do you know of Christian persecution around the world today? What do you think when you read verses like 2 Timothy 3:12? Comment on Tyndale's courage in the face of physical brutality and discuss the connection between courage, belief, prudence, and trust of other people.

3. What was Tyndale's view of lay people? Where did the distinction between the laity and the clergy begin? Is it a healthy view? Why or why not?

4. Tyndale was a man of vast learning. Why are brilliant thinkers necessary in the church? Comment on Tyndale's treatment of those with less education. Comment on the necessity of teachers who know their material and are able to articulate it clearly and simply.

5. Christian businessmen helped Tyndale with their financial resources. Read Luke 8:1–3, and comment on Jesus' experience. What role should businesspeople play in today's Christian ministries?

Name

>William Tyndale Today

6 Gutenberg's printing press was essential to the supernatural success of the gospel; many people ' received the good news quickly. Discuss whether or not Christians should use television, radio, and the Internet. Compare the written word with the visual image. Which is more powerful? Why? If you had to choose between the two, which would you choose? Explain.

_____

_____

_____

7 Tyndale was betrayed by Henry Phillips, a man who had befriended him. In Jesus' case, Judas and his betrayal of Jesus were providentially planned. But in wisdom, how do we keep our distance from those who would harm us? How can Christians be "wise as serpents but innocent as doves"? Reread 2 Timothy 2:14–26.

_____

_____

_____

8 How should people respond to corruption in the church today as Tyndale did in his day? Is it possible to see ourselves for who we really are, acknowledging our own sinfulness while looking out for "wolves in sheeps' clothing"? (Matthew 7 and Acts 20)

_____

_____

_____

9 Read Romans 15:14–22. Do you know of anyone with the same kind of focus and zealousness? How would you respond to people like Tyndale? Would you write them off as arrogant or intractable? Would you follow them? Would you acknowledge the sacrifices made by such people, or would you consider them fools, so heavenly minded that they are no earthly good? Why?

_____

_____

_____

>Mother Tongues and Elephant Ears

The Hebrew language is . . .

1 a language of economy

Psalm 23 has more than a hundred words in any English translation; in Hebrew, Psalm 23 has only fifty-five words. Hebrew is a language of few words. Why is that true? Adjectives, for example, are simply doubled nouns in Hebrew: "double heart [flattering lips]" (Psalm 12:2) or "deep [tar] pits" (Genesis 14:10). (Tell students that the Hebrew literally reads *pits-pits*, as in "There are pits, and then there are pits!")

Write some other examples:

Song of Solomon 1:1 _____

Isaiah 6:3 _____

Isaiah 26:3 _____

2 a language of emotion

In 1 Samuel 20:30, Saul uses profanity against Jonathan. The Hebrew records the outburst without blushing; English translations soften it: "You son of a perverse and rebellious woman!" Discourse in Hebrew is direct rather than indirect.

Read Genesis 3:9–13 and write down language of emotion and directness:

_____

_____

_____

_____

3 a language of action

Normally, the order of a Hebrew sentence is verb, subject, object: for example, *Joshua ran the race* would be, in Hebrew, *Ran Joshua the race*. Putting the verb first reflects the action-centered lifestyle of the people. (A King James Bible would be best for this exercise since it is a more word-for-word translation of the Hebrew.) For example: to look is to "lift up the eyes": in Genesis 22:4, Abraham "lifted his eyes." To be angry is to "burn one's nostrils" or similar: in Exodus 4:14, God's anger "was kindled."

Read the following verses for more examples. (If possible, compare the verses in the New International version with the same ones in the original King James version or the NKJV.)

Ruth 4:4 _____

1 Samuel 6:6 _____

2 Chronicles 30:8 _____

Jeremiah 1:17 _____

Jeremiah 42:15 _____

Name

>Mother Tongues and Elephant Ears

Even in an English translation we sense progression and constant movement. How many times is *and* used to begin a sentence in Genesis 1:2–3:1?

④ a language of word pictures

"The apple of His eye" (Deuteronomy 32:10) and "escaped by the skin of my teeth" (Job 19:20) are two of the most familiar of hundreds of metaphors and other figurative expressions translated directly from the Hebrew.

Using a King James Bible, find a figure of speech in each verse and explain its meaning. For some verses, looking them up in the New International Bible as well will help you find the literal meaning of a metaphor.

Isaiah 47:3

_____

_____

Proverbs 4:20

_____

_____

Psalm 57

_____

_____

Psalm 125:5

_____

Ecclesiastes 12:11

_____

_____

Isaiah 1:18

_____

_____

Nahum 3:5

_____

_____

Psalm 73:2

_____

>Mother Tongues
and Elephant Ears

5 a language of the physical

The Hebrew people conceive of their mental and emotional states as located in their bodily organs, reflecting their belief that a human being was a whole, an indivisible entity.

For each emotion, find the physical part or organ that the writer suggests is involved:

sadness: Job 16:15

_____

worship: Psalm 35:10

_____

depression: Genesis 4:6

_____

bless: Numbers 6:25

_____

stress, tension: Job 30:27

_____

sorrow; despair: Lamentations 2:11

_____

_____

6 a language of earthiness

Some people (and cultures) tend to be reserved about certain subjects. The Hebrews were direct in identifying the common stuff of life.

Discover a few examples of direct writing:

Isaiah 36:12 _____

Isaiah 64:6 _____

Jeremiah 2:24 _____

Name

1 Coining the Koine

The word *koine* means:

_____

_____

_____

Greek is a language of:

a _____

_____

_____

b _____

_____

_____

c _____

_____

_____

d _____

_____

_____

Name

>It's All
   Greek To Me!

② Pieces of Papyrus

_____

a▷ "Give us this day our daily bread" (Luke 11:1, 2)

_____

_____

b▷ "They have their reward" (Matthew 6:2, 5)

_____

_____

c▷ "They should take nothing . . . no scrip" (Mark 6:8)

_____

_____

d▷ "Labor in vain" (1 Corinthians 15:58)

_____

_____

e▷ "Chief shepherd" (1 Peter 5:4)

_____

_____

f▷ "Co-heirs with Christ" (Romans 8:17)

_____

_____

g▷ "Blotting out" (Colossians 2:14)

_____

_____

3 Why This Matters to Us

a ▶
_____
_____
_____

b ▶
_____
_____
_____

c ▶
_____
_____
_____

d ▶
_____
_____
_____

e ▶
_____
_____
_____

Name

① Early Translations

Translation means:

Remember John Wycliffe?
   What he believed:

_____

_____

   What he did:

_____

_____

_____

What was the main difference in how Wycliffe's and Tyndale's Bibles were translated?

Wycliffe
Hebrew/Greek Original
▼
Latin
▼
English

Tyndale
Hebrew/Greek Original
▼
English

Note that Tyndale's work was more directly from the original.

② Translations and Paraphrases

Compare the following translations from the book of Job, noting their strengths and weaknesses.

With clouds he covereth the light; and commandeth it not to shine by the cloud that cometh betwixt. The noise thereof sheweth concerning it, the cattle also concerning the vapour (KJV).

_____

_____

_____

He fills his hands with lightning bolts. He hurls each at its target. We feel his presence in the thunder. May all sinners be warned (LB).

_____

_____

_____

>Translation and Paraphrase

List the differences between a paraphrase, a word-for-word translation, and a thought-for-thought translation.

PARAPHRASE	WORD-FOR-WORD	THOUGHT-FOR-THOUGHT
Example: Living Bible (LB) Idea-for-idea English Some slang More readable Less accurate, or faithful to the original languages Good for overview study	Example: New American Standard (NASB) Word for word Formal English Less readable More accurate, or faithful to the original languages Good for detailed study	Example: New International Version (NIV) "Dynamic equivalent": the thought of the verse in its context Everyday English More readable than word-for-word More accurate to the original languages than a paraphrase Good for either overview or detailed study

What word in the Interact title denotes the Bible used in this class? _____

Find the five verses below, and find a word or phrase that is translated differently in some of them:

	1 Samuel 20:30	Job 40:15	1 Kings 18:27	Matthew 18:24	Galatians 3:24
KJV	perverse and rebellious	behemoth	talking, pursuing in a journey sleepeth	ten thousand talents	schoolmaster
NKJV	SAME	SAME	meditating, busy, on a journey, sleeping	SAME	tutor
NASB	SAME	SAME	occupied or busy	SAME	SAME
NIV	SAME	SAME	deep in thought, busy, traveling, sleeping	SAME	put in charge
RSV	SAME	SAME	asleep, meditation journey	SAME	custodian, disciplinarian
LB	S.O.B.	SAME	talking or sitting on the toilet	$10 million	teacher
GNB/ TEV	bastard	monster	talking or relieving himself	millions	in charge

Discuss which Bibles are best for you, and why.

• For overview reading: _____

• For detailed study: _____

>You Be the Checker

Ready to test your translation skills with some puzzles? Imagine that you know nothing about the Bible, and a translator has just moved in next door. He asks you to help check a translation of the Bible in your language, English.

"I don't know," you say, slightly curious but unsure of your language expertise. "Maybe you should ask John Doe. He's an A student."

"No," the translator replies. "John Doe was on the translation team with me. Now I need someone else to check it. All I need is someone who speaks English."

Your curiosity gets the better of you, and you agree to help. "Now remember," the translator says, "I'm primarily concerned with naturalness. Tell me which of these two choices communicates more clearly to you. What makes each choice different? Which is easier to understand?"

Luke 7:44

I entered your house, and you gave me no water for my feet.
I came into your house but you provided no water to wash my feet.

What's the difference between these two translations? Which is easier to understand?

Mark 1:2

It began as the prophet Isaiah had written: "Here is my messenger," says God; "I will send him ahead of you to open the way for you."

As it is written in Isaiah the prophet, "See, I am sending my messenger before thy face, who will prepare the way."

What's the difference between these two? Which is easier to understand?

Luke 17:26

As it was in the days of Noah, so will it be in the days of the Son of Man.
In the time of the coming of the Son of Man, life will be as it was in the days of Noah.

What's the difference between these two? Which is easier to understand?

"Thank you," the translator says, "that was a big help. Could you help me with something else?"

You check your watch and notice that your favorite TV show isn't coming on for another half an hour. "Sure," you reply.

"Great. I'd like to check several idioms—you know, figures of speech peculiar to English. Like saying 'cold shoulder' or 'green with envy.' John Doe used some English idioms when we were translating, and I'm not familiar with them. What do they mean?"

Acts 13:36—David . . . fell asleep, and was laid with his fathers.
Natural meaning:

Acts 7:60—And when he had said this, he fell asleep.
Natural meaning:

Acts 22:22—Away with such a fellow from the earth!
Natural meaning:

Luke 2:5—Mary was with child.
Natural meaning:

Acts 18:6—Your blood be upon your heads!
Natural meaning:

Mark 10:22—His countenance fell.
Natural meaning:

When you told the translator that the natural meaning of the first example was, "David died and was buried with his ancestors," his eyes lit up and he scribbled something down in his notebook.

"You are doing great," he says. "Can you help with one last thing?"

By now you're enjoying yourself, so you don't mind missing a few minutes of your show. You've never looked at your own language in this way before!

"John Doe translated these passages for me," the translator says. He used the same word, *spirit,* in each, but I know that word has several different meanings. Would you check what he did and make sure it's good English usage? Could you also match the meanings I've listed with the correct verses?

> demon, evil spirit
> angel, good spirit
> Spirit of God, Holy Spirit
> part of the human personality
> ghost, spirit of a dead person

>You Be the Checker

Mark 5:13 The unclean spirits came out and entered the swine.

Correct definition: _____

Hebrews 1:14 Are they not all ministering spirits sent forth to serve?

Correct definition: _____

Acts 2:4 They began to speak in other tongues as the Spirit gave them utterance.

Correct definition: _____

Matthew 26:41 The spirit indeed is willing, but the flesh is weak.

Correct definition: _____

Acts 16:16 We were met by a slave girl who had a spirit of divination and brought her owners much gain by soothsaying.

Correct definition: _____

Luke 24:37 But they were startled and frightened and supposed that they saw a spirit.

Correct definition: _____

Galatians 3:2 Did you receive the Spirit by the works of the law, or by hearing with faith?

Correct definition: _____

Luke 1:80 And the child grew and became strong in spirit.

Correct definition: _____

Name

"That's all I have today," the translator says, making a mental note to come to you again since you've been so helpful.

"Come back any time," you tell him. And you also make a mental note to read the translation he's working on with John Doe, once it's completed.

Carol Chase, "You Be the Checker," from *In Other Words*, vol. 10, no. 3. © 1983; Wycliffe Bible Translators, Huntington Beach, CA; revised March 2000

>Illumination

Illumination means that:

_____

_____

_____

Write down the key ingredients to
illumination found in 1 John 2:20–27:

_____

_____

_____

_____

_____

_____

_____

In a poem:

Light *obeyed* increases *light*.
Light *rejected* brings on *night*.

Illumination might be pictured this way:

The Holy Spirit → Teacher / Individual → Scripture → Teaching Others

Look up the following Scriptures to find out how people can put out illumination:

1 Corinthians 2:14 _____

Psalm 66:18 _____

2 Peter 2:1 _____

1 Thessalonians 5:19–22 _____

Look up the following Scriptures to discover who and what are illuminated:

Psalm 18:28 _____

Psalm 19:8 _____

Psalm 119:18 _____

Luke 24:32 _____

Luke 24:45 _____

Acts 16:14 _____

2 Corinthians 13:3 _____

2 Corinthians 4:6 _____

Ephesians 1:18 _____

Ephesians 3:16 _____

Name

>Illumination

Complete the chart. Use your notes and 1 Corinthians 2:7–13 to discover some differences between revelation, inspiration, and illumination.

	Revelation	Inspiration	Illumination
To whom given			
What is given			
When it is given			
How it is given			
Which verses in 1 Cor. 2			

So what? Who cares? Why study this today? Why is illumination important? With a partner or a small group, evaluate how this teaching should apply to every Christian. Think about how illumination can be applied positively or misused negatively.

_____

_____

_____

_____

_____

_____

_____

_____

>An Illumination Workout

"Test the spirits to see if they're from God" (1 John 4:1). Compare the idea in each statement on the left with the Scriptures next to it. In column three, tell how the statement contradicts Scripture and is therefore false. Later, in a class discussion, note any sect or religion that embraces that false teaching.

Belief Statement	Scripture	Why False?
Blessed are those who purify their consciousness; they shall see themselves as God. (Zen Buddhism)	Matthew 5:8 Romans 11:33–36	
Jesus is the firstborn of all creation (Col. 1:15). Therefore, He was created and is not God. (Jehovah's Witnesses)	Colossians 1:15–17 Hebrews 1:10–13	
They misbelieve who say, "verily, God is the third of three." "They slew him not and they crucified him not, that they had only his likeness." (Islam: Koran)	Matthew 28:19 2 Corinthians 13:14 Matthew 27:35–40 Acts 2:22–24	
Through reincarnation, all humans reap the good or bad consequences of their actions. One's position in the next life depends on what one does in this life. (Eastern religions)	Hebrews 9:27 Matthew 10:28 Luke 13:16–21	
All things are one. There is no difference between good and bad, God and humans; all things are part of the whole. (Hinduism)	Genesis 1:1 Psalm 104:27–30 Matthew 13:35–37	
Jesus' message was good for His time. Baha'u'llah came later, and his message was fuller and better than Jesus' message. (Baha'i)	Hebrews 10:13 Ephesians 1:7 Hebrews 9:26–28	

Name

110

>Interpretation

1 Biblical interpretation is:

_____

_____

2 What are the qualifications for interpreting the Bible according to these verses?

Scriptures	Qualifications: A Bible interpreter must be . . .
John 3:6; 1 Corinthians 2:14, 15	
Jeremiah 15:16; 1 Peter 2:2	
James 4:6–10	
Ephesians 1:18	

3 Second Timothy 2:15 contains key phrases about what an interpreter should do. Complete the verse, and discuss with the class the meaning of each phrase you wrote.

Do your best to _____ as one approved, a _____

who does not need to be ashamed and who _____ the word of truth.

4 Is THIS Interpretation? What views of Bible interpretation are expressed or implied in each statement below. Discuss with the class how Bible interpretation should and should not be accomplished.

* My Bible fell open and my finger went a pokin. _____

* A chapter a day keeps Satan away. _____

* Read clear through in a year or two. _____

* I'll find a verse, and then we'll converse. _____

5 Seeing is not always believing! Read John 20:1–9, and list four verses that mention or imply seeing. The verse numbers are _____

Three people saw, but only one "saw and believed." When we read Scripture, we need to do more than see; we should _____

Name

>An Interpretation
Workout

Read a Scripture verse and a possible interpretation. Tell what seems to be wrong or overemphasized in each interpretation.

Scripture	Interpretation	What's Wrong?
Judges 6:36–40	Gideon made his decision by putting out a fleece. I will use the same method of decision-making, devising my own test.	
2 Chronicles 7:14	The verse refers to the United States. If Americans will repent of their sin, they will again be God's chosen people.	
Proverbs 3:9, 10	God wants us to be healthy and wealthy.	
Matthew 18:20	Where two or three are gathered, they can worship God—anytime and anywhere—so I'll just skip church and worship God in the great outdoors.	
Romans 9:21	Some people are physically attractive, but others are ordinary.	
1 Thessalonians 5:22	We should avoid every appearance of evil, so we should not be seen with unbelievers.	
James 1:2–7	When I need answers on a test, God will give them to me.	
Revelation 3:20	Jesus is waiting for unbelievers to decide to accept or reject Him.	

Name

>Cancer Grows,
Gangrene Spreads

Read with your classmates the following passages in 2 Timothy, and answer the questions below.

1 According to each passage, what are the dangers of false interpretation?

a 2 Timothy 2:16–18

_____

_____

_____

b 2 Timothy 4:3–5

_____

_____

_____

2 Paul tells Timothy the proper responses to false interpretation. What are they?

a 2 Timothy 2:15–26

_____

_____

_____

_____

_____

b 2 Timothy 3:14–4:5

_____

_____

_____

_____

_____

_____

_____

_____

Name

>Agreeing to Disagree

1 Major on the _____

Read, then write, what 1 Corinthians 15:1–6 says is essential Christian truth.

_____

_____

_____

2 Allow the Bible to speak _____

Beware of your own theological

Read and discuss the problem of personal perspectives in 1 Corinthians 3:1–9.

_____

_____

_____

3 One cannot simply dismiss something from Scripture as if it doesn't _____
Read Acts 13:46–48 and record the two seemingly contradictory statements that appear in the same context.

_____

_____

_____

4 Christians may not always _____
Record Jesus' comment in Mark 9:38–41 about those with whom we disagree.

_____

Record what Scripture says about quarreling: Proverbs 13:10; 15:18; 17:14, 19; 20:3; 22:10; 26:17, 20; 1Corinthians 1:11; 3:3; 2 Corinthians 12:20; 1 Timothy 3:3; 2 Timothy 2:23; James 4:2. Are these Scriptures teaching us that Christians should agree about everything? Explain.

_____

5 _____ is not allowed!

Explain what Scripture says in 1 Timothy 1:4 and 6:4, and in Titus 3:9–11 about controversies over minutia.

_____

_____

_____

Name

>To Beg,
Borrow, or Steal

1 Analyze the three statements below, answering the questions for each.

Hammurabi's law code (c. 1750 B.C.) protected property by punishing the thief by (a) execution, (b) restitution twentyfold, or (c) indentured slavery. Civilizations before the Hebrews brought law and order to their lands without a revelation from God.

● According to Exodus 22:1–9, what was the amount of restitution demanded in Israel for theft?

_____

● What principle is established in Leviticus 24:19, 20 about punishment and the offender?

_____

● What is the distinction between Hammurabi's law and the Mosaic law concerning people and property? Why is that important?

_____

_____

The Hebrews took their ideas on kingship from surrounding cultures. There was no difference between believers and unbelievers in the institution of kingship.

● What does God warn the Israelites concerning the institution of kingship in 1 Samuel 8:10–18?

_____

● Why was it important for the king to practice the mandate in Deuteronomy 17:15–20?

_____

● Read Psalm 24 and comment on the similarities, but more importantly the differences, between nation states in the ancient Near East.

_____

_____

The gods of Canaan, Egypt, and Babylon had the same powers and titles ascribed to them as did the Hebrew God. Thus these deities were all made by humans.

● Review the names for God in **Interact 8.2 Canonization**. Why is this difference important?

_____

● Other nations claimed holiness for their priests, places, and books but not for their gods. How, then, did a description like the one in Isaiah 6 set the God of Scripture apart?

_____

_____

_____

● Discuss some questions that are left unanswered if humans create their "god." Why are these important?

_____

_____

Name

2 Discuss the following statements, explaining why you agree or disagree. Give reasons for your answer

When we observe parallel concepts in different cultures, we realize that:

The Bible is a man-made book. ———————————————————————————

The Bible depends on the culture. ———————————————————————————

The Bible writers copied other books. ———————————————————————————

The Bible's words mean the same as those of other cultures.

———————————————————————————

———————————————————————————

3 Discuss the following statements, reading the Scripture for each:

 "Beware of 'Americanizing' Christianity." Skim Acts 15:19–35. What was important? What was peripheral?

———————————————————————————

"The method of Bible communication may change depending on the groups being addressed."

Skim Acts 13–17 to see what people or groups were addressed by Paul and how he may have tailored his approach to each audience.

———————————————————————————

———————————————————————————

———————————————————————————

"We should not find Bible verses to defend a position we have taken on some cultural issue." Review the ideas in unit 13 about interpretation. Should we allow the Bible to speak for itself or read what we want to into the Bible?

———————————————————————————

"Christians can learn from their culture." Luke 16:1–8 and Acts 17:28 teach this very idea. Jesus sai that unbelievers were shrewder than believers; Paul quoted a pagan poet. Christians must realize that all truth is God's truth no matter who says it or where it comes from.

>Loose the Chains

Did the Old Testament laws governing or restricting slavery assume slavery to be ethically correct?

1 Slavery was practiced for societal reasons resulting from:

- _____
- _____
- _____

2 The laws regarding slavery, in both testaments, highlight:

_____

a Law was conditioned by _____

- **Exodus 23:9**   **Leviticus 25:42, 46, 53, 55**   **Deuteronomy 15:15**

Because Israel had been enslaved, Israelites could not be enslaved for life.

b So because Israel "knew what it felt like,"

- The law protected the slave from his or her _____

  The slave was either _____ if killed (Exodus 21:20, 21)

  or _____ for loss (Exodus 21:26–27).

- The law protected the slave from _____ (Deuteronomy 15:13–16).

  The concern was for the slave's _____

- The law provided for _____ (Deuteronomy 23:15–16).

  Other societies punished both the _____ and the _____

- The law included the slave in

- Deuteronomy 16:11–15 _____
- Exodus 12:44 _____
- Exodus 20:10 _____

c Slavery was _unnatural_ (in no way essential).

- **Genesis 9:25–27**   **Proverbs 17:5**   **Proverbs 14:31**
- **Job 31:13–15**   **Proverbs 29:13**

People were considered

_____

_____

_____

Name

>The Authority of the Bible

(1) What authority figures do you listen to? Tell *why* you listen to each one.

_____

_____

_____

_____

(2) What are three basic kinds of authority? List the problems with each.

The authority of Scripture means:

_____

_____

a _____

Problem: _____

b _____

Problem: _____

c _____

Problem: _____

Is there a solution?

_____

_____

_____

(3) Where did we come from? How did we get here? Why should I accept the Bible as my personal basis for authority?

Scripture's historical documentation. → Scripture reveals Jesus as God-Man. → Jesus taught that the Scripture is inspired. → **therefore** → If I obey Jesus, I come under Jesus' authority; and since Jesus' authority is found in Scripture, I come under Scripture's authority.

Write what each verse says about Jesus' authority.

a Matthew 5:17 _____

b Matthew 9:6, 8 _____

c Matthew 28:18 _____

d Mark 1:22 _____

>How Would You Respond?

6 A college student explains, "Of course I dislike the Nazis, but who's to say that they're morally wrong?"

Problem: _____

Solution: _____

7 A church takes a survey of the community and discovers that words such as *redemption, conversion, sin,* and *guilt* are either misunderstood or are turning people off. In response, the church leadership does away with all difficult or unpleasant teaching. Many more people begin coming to the church.

Problem: _____

Solution: _____

8 A psychologist describes a murderer's behavior this way: "He's misunderstood. The poor home environment in which he grew up produced miscommunication and rebellion. The word *evil* is too harsh to describe him. He's simply exhibiting irresponsible behavior in response to negative stimuli."

Problem: _____

Solution: _____

9 A sociologist reports, "Some people may be superior to others, while all viewpoints are equal."

Problem: _____

Solution: _____

10 A philosopher concludes, "Once the reality of an absolute is denied, all arguments, all human relationships, are nothing more than an exercise in power."

Problem: _____

Solution: _____

>How Would You Respond?

For each case study identify the problem and propose a solution:

1 A comedian is asked, "Is there anything that's in poor taste to joke about?" He responds, "When I tell a joke and 2,000 people laugh, the joke is in good taste. If they don't laugh, it's in poor taste."

Problem: _____

_____

Solution: _____

_____

2 A famous personality says, "I hope my choices please people, but I make choices to please myself."

Problem: _____

_____

Solution: _____

_____

3 A writer declares, "Fact and truth are not the same; some of the Bible is history, and some of the Bible is story. We don't always know which is which, but it doesn't matter."

Problem: _____

_____

Solution: _____

_____

4 *Metallica* (a rock band) plays a song entitled "Eye of the Beholder," in which the lyrics include, "Do you need what I need? Boundaries overthrown. Look inside to each his own. Do you trust what I trust? Me, myself, and I."

Problem: _____

_____

Solution: _____

_____

5 A panel of educational experts reports, "After years of research, we have decided that instructors are presumptuous if they assume they have the 'truth' on a subject. Truth may change tomorrow. In addition, telling students their answer isn't 'true' may damage their self-esteem."

Problem: _____

_____

Solution: _____

_____

Name

>How Would You Respond?

6 A college student explains, "Of course I dislike the Nazis, but who's to say that they're morally wrong?

Problem: _____

_____

Solution: _____

_____

7 A church takes a survey of the community and discovers that words such as *redemption, conversion, sin,* and *guilt* are either misunderstood or are turning people off. In response, the church leadership does away with all difficult or unpleasant teaching. Many more people begin coming to the church.

Problem: _____

_____

Solution: _____

_____

8 A psychologist describes a murderer's behavior this way: "He's misunderstood. The poor home environment in which he grew up produced miscommunication and rebellion. The word *evil* is too harsh to describe him. He's simply exhibiting irresponsible behavior in response to negative stimuli."

Problem: _____

_____

Solution: _____

_____

9 A sociologist reports, "Some people may be superior to others, while all viewpoints are equal."

Problem: _____

_____

Solution: _____

_____

10 A philosopher concludes, "Once the reality of an absolute is denied, all arguments, all human relationships, are nothing more than an exercise in power."

Problem: _____

_____

Solution: _____

_____

>Mythology and Genesis

Similarities and Differences

1 What is a myth?

Definition _____

Popularizer _____

2 What principles are held by those who say the Bible is myth?

_____

_____

_____

_____

_____

_____

3 Why do people say that the Bible is myth?

Parallel accounts _____

_____

Similarities _____

_____

The general belief _____

_____

Name

4 How might we respond to similarities?

Similarities are not:

_____

_____

_____

Similarity does not mean:

_____

_____

_____

_____

5 What are some key ways in which the Akkadian and Alaskan creation myths differ from the creation account in Genesis?

_____

_____

_____

_____

_____

_____

_____

_____

_____

_____

_____

_____

_____

_____

1 Important distinctions between myths and Genesis:

a ▷ **The** _____ **of the gods**

The ancient Near Eastern gods were trapped in their own ethical dilemmas.
They were anything but upstanding examples of righteous behavior! Only Yahweh ("LORD" in NIV)
is referred to as _____

b ▷ **The** _____ **of the gods**

The gods were created and were therefore finite. Their finiteness contrasts with

_____

Also, notice how much the gods of mythology resemble *humans.* Contrast the ancient Near Eastern
concept with that of the Hebrew Old Testament, in which humans were

_____

c ▷ **The** _____ **origin of the universe**

In contrast with the Hebrew belief, other ancient Near Eastern cultures believed that matter was

_____

Of the various creation accounts, only Genesis uses the word

_____

2 A proposed solution to the origin of the creation myths:

Genesis 1 and 2

**The true, pure words of
God given to humans
explaining how the
universe originated
directly through the
personal eternal Creator.**

Genesis 3

In spite of sin's distortion, pieces of truth concerning the
origin of the universe remained. However, human corruption
twisted the original details of time, place, God, man,
and creation, accounting for such myths as the *Enuma Elish.*

Mesopotamian
creation story
Enuma Elish

Alaskan
creation
story

Egyptian
creation story

Appendix
>Supplementary Readings

Supplementary Readings

The following lessons require the use of the excerpts that follow, which are reprinted with permission.

Lesson 2.1

Susan Schaeffer Macaulay, "Cliff-hanger"

Rebecca Manley Pippert, from *Hope Has Its Reasons*

Lesson 4.3

Susan Schaeffer Macaulay, "Lost in the Forest"

Lesson 6.4

Bo Lozoff, "Letter from God"

Lesson 7.1

Jeffery L. Sheler, "What Did Jesus Really Say?"

Richard N. Ostling, "Jesus Christ, Plain and Simple"

Lesson 12.2

Neil Anderson and Hyatt Moore, from *In Search of the Source*: Chapter 16, "Broken Bodies"; Chapter 18, "Payback"; Chapter 19, "Ransom"

Lesson 14.2

C. W. Powell, "Unbiblical Blackjack"

Lesson 14.4

Douglas Wilson, "Remade in Our Image"

Lesson 17.1

"Enuma Elish," from *Primal Myths*, ed. by Barbara C. Sproul

Cliff-hanger

If you were to visit L'Abri, you might hear an imaginary story that my father [Francis Schaeffer] often includes in his teaching.

He asks you to suppose that you are lost in the Alps. Your view of the steep cliffs beneath you disappears into the fog. Night comes. Ice forms. It is death to carry on climbing.

You cling to the ledge with numbed fingers, and speak to your friend. "If we stay here, we will be dead by morning. I think we should jump into the darkness. Maybe there is a ledge below. If there is one, maybe we could have shelter until dawn. We will die anyway on this ledge."

That kind of jump would be a blind leap of faith.

But there is a second possibility. Imagine that you are on the same icy cliff. Fog swirls. Death approaches. Suddenly, from away over the pass, a voice shouts out of the darkness: "I can see that you are stuck on the cliff. You can't see me, but I see just where you are. I am a Swiss guide, and I know that if you jump in a certain direction there is a safe, sheltered ledge below you. There you will be able to stay until morning, when I can come and get you."

Aha! This is a different situation. You can question the speaker. Is he reliable? Test his statements. Check out the facts. Then, finally, if you choose to, jump. It is still foggy, and you can't see if what the guide says is true. But it is not a blind leap of faith anymore.

In the same way, you don't have to blindly believe in the Bible. You can ask questions and test the answers. You can see if it fits reality. You can see if it's true, reliable, sure—and worth putting your trust in.

> Susan Schaeffer Macaulay. "Cliff-hanger," *How to Be Your Own Selfish Pig*. Cook Communications, 1982.

From: Hope Has Its Reasons

During an out-of-town speaking engagement, I was staying in the home of a woman whom I will call Catherine. I asked her how she came to faith. She said that she had a vague Episcopalian background and went to church on the holidays, but faith was never a personal issue for her. Slowly she began to feel that something was missing in her life. She had everything she could wish for materially by the world's standards, yet she felt an undefined emptiness.

At the same time, she began to notice there was something remarkable about her maid Ruby. Ruby had been coming to her home for ten years; she was part of the family. Ruby always radiated a calm and joy that Catherine envied. She noticed that Ruby would sing hymns while she washed the kitchen floors. Why would anyone want to sing when they did something as menial as wash a floor? The more Catherine observed her behavior, the more intrigued she became as to the source of Ruby's peace. So she asked Ruby to tell her the secret of her contentment and Ruby shared her faith. Eventually Catherine decided to be a follower of Jesus too. But the part of the story that really struck me was to follow.

Suddenly Catherine began to have trouble with her teenage daughter. She got a call from the police that her daughter had been arrested for breaking into a neighbor's house and stealing jewelry. She had cocaine in her purse when they arrested her. Catherine came back from the county jail devastated and weeping. She began to tell Ruby what had happened.

"Ruby, what am I going to do? How can I help her? It may be too late! I am absolutely distraught," she sobbed.

Ruby said, "Child, Jesus already died for your daughter, there's no need for you to die, too."

"But, Ruby," Catherine protested, "you don't understand. I have prayed for her and nothing has happened."

"And how long have you been praying for your child?" Ruby asked.

"For at least six months, ever since I came to faith," Catherine answered.

"And how long have I been working for you?" Ruby asked.

"Ten years," Catherine answered.

"That's right! And for nine years and six months I have been on my knees washing these floors and praying for the salvation of this home! And did you hear me complain because it took so long? Don't you rush Jesus, girl! You give him room, be patient, and pray."

"You call that piddly stuff I hear you do prayin'?" Ruby asked.

"But, Ruby, you don't understand, I am desperate!" Catherine pleaded.

"Now we're talkin' prayer! You let Ruby teach you how to pray. The cleaning can wait. Do you have a Bible?" Ruby asked.

Now Catherine was puzzled because she knew that Ruby couldn't read. She quickly got a Bible, although she was afraid that Ruby might feel embarrassed. But to her surprise, Ruby began walking around the house and in her beautiful deep voice she lifted her arms and prayed the Psalms, word for word. She started, and her voice crescendoed: "He who dwells in the shelter of the Most High, who abides in the shadow of the Almighty, will say to the Lord, 'My refuge and my fortress; my God, in whom I will trust.'" Then she would turn to Catherine, tell her which psalm she was quoting, and then she was off on another one. I have a mental picture of it; Ruby, calmly, jubilantly striding through the house as she prayed; Catherine, frantically trying to keep up with her.

The next day as I was leaving, Ruby came in, having just arrived by bus. We spoke at the kitchen table, and I told her how moved I was by her influence in that home. "Oh, Becky, if you only knew how I have grieved for the poverty in this home!" Ruby said, as I sat and listened amidst Baccarat crystal, Persian rugs, and priceless antiques.

That is the difference the resurrection makes. That is how Jesus has "thrown everything off balance." Jesus turns everything upside down. For who would have guessed, walking into that home for the first time, who was the teacher and who the student, who was the literate and who the illiterate, who was the wealthy and who the poor?

Following Jesus is living life from a new angle, living life with a new energy resource. And the different angle and power he offers has been opened up by the resurrection. We can become "resurrection people" like Ruby. Ruby's last words as I left were, "But Jesus is winnin' and there's a new song to sing." A new song to sing indeed.

> Reprinted from *Hope Has Its Reasons* by Rebecca Manley Pippert. © 1989 by Rebecca Manley Pippert. Used by permission of InterVarsity Press, PO Box 1400, Downers Grove, IL 60515.

Lost in the Forest

Imagine that you are hiking through a great forest, and lose your way. A storm sets in. You're relieved to see a hut in a clearing. A light shines from the window, and smoke curls from the chimney. You practically run to the door, hoping to find shelter there.

You knock. No answer.

You call. No voice replies.

You go to the window to look in. What a relief! The hut is occupied. There is a fire burning, and a kettle bubbling merrily over it. The table is set for supper, and a freshly baked pie sits in the center.

What do you know about this setting, using scientific observation? You know that someone lives in this hut, even though no one is home at the moment.

Someone had to have built the fire, put water in the kettle, set the table, and baked the pie. From the state of things, you gather that the person will come back soon to eat the supper he's prepared. You are not alone in the forest.

You cannot see the owner of the hut any more than you can see God or angels. Yet the evidence of that owner's existence seems overwhelming.

Try looking at the world as you did that imaginary hut in the forest. Do you see evidence of the hand of a Creator? Is the evidence as convincing as you would like it to be? Is there somebody at home in the universe?

> Susan Schaeffer Macaulay. "Lost in the Forest," *How to Be Your Own Selfish Pig*. Cook Communications, 1982.

Lesson 6.4

Letter from God

From: GOD

To: My Children on Earth

Re: Idiotic Religious Rivalries

My Dear Children (and believe me, that's all of you),

I consider myself a pretty patient guy. I mean, look at the Grand Canyon. It took millions of years to get it right. And about evolution? Boy, nothing is slower than designing that whole Darwinian thing to take place, cell by cell, and gene by gene.

I've been patient through your fashions, civilizations, wars and schemes, and the countless ways you take Me for granted until you get yourselves into big trouble again and again.

I want to let you know about some of the things that are starting to tick Me off.

First of all, your religious rivalries are driving Me up a wall. Enough already! Let's get one thing straight! These are YOUR religions, not Mine.

I'm the whole enchilada; I'm beyond them all. Every one of your religions claims there is only one of Me (which, by the way, is absolutely true).

But in the very next breath, each religion claims it's My favorite one. And each claims its bible was written personally by Me, and that all the other bibles are man-made. Oh, Me. How do I even begin to put a stop to such complicated nonsense?

Okay, listen up now. I'm your Father AND Mother, and I don't play favorites among My children. Also, I hate to break it to you, but I don't write. So ALL of your books, including those bibles, were written by men and women. They were inspired men and women, they were remarkable people, but they also made mistakes here and there. I made sure of that, so that you would never trust a written word rather than your own living heart.

You see, one human being to Me—even a bum on the street—is worth more than all the holy books in the world. That's just the kind of guy I am. My Spirit is not a historical thing. It's alive right here, right now, as fresh as your next breath.

Holy books and religious rites are sacred and powerful, but not more so than the least of you. They were only meant to steer you in the right direction, not to keep you arguing with each other, and certainly not to keep you from trusting your own personal connection with Me.

Which brings Me to My next point about your nonsense. You act like I need you and your religions to stick up for Me or "win souls" for My sake. Please, don't do Me any favors. I can stand quite well on My own, thank you. I don't need you to defend Me, and I don't need constant credit. I just want you to be good to each other.

And another thing: I don't get all worked up over money or politics, so stop dragging My name into your dramas. For example, I swear to Me that I never threatened Oral Roberts. I never rode in any of Rajneesh's Rolls Royces. I never told Pat Robertson to run for president, and I've never EVER had a conversation with Jim Bakker, Jerry Falwell, or Jimmy Swaggert! Of course, come Judgment Day, I certainly intend to…

The thing is, I want you to stop thinking of religion as some sort of loyalty pledge to Me. The true purpose of your religions is so that YOU can become more aware of ME, not the other way around. Believe Me, I know you already. I know what's in each of your hearts, and I love you with no strings attached. Lighten up and enjoy Me. That's what religion is best for.

What you seem to forget is how mysterious I am. You look at the petty differences in your Scriptures and say, "Well, if THIS is the truth, then THAT can't be!" But instead of trying to figure out My Paradoxes and Unfathomable Nature—which, by the way, you NEVER will—why not open your hearts to the simple common threads in all religions?

You know what I'm talking about: Love and respect everyone. Be kind, even when life is scary or confusing, take courage and be of good cheer, for I am always with you. Learn how to be quiet, so you can hear My still, small voice (I don't like to shout). Leave the world a better place by living your life with dignity and gracefulness, for you are My Own Child. Hold back nothing from life, for the parts of you that can die surely will, and the parts that can't, won't. So don't worry, be happy (I stole that last line from Bobby McFerrin, but who do you think gave it to him in the first place?).

Simple stuff. Why do you keep making it so complicated? It's like you're always looking for an excuse to be upset. And I'm very tired of being your main excuse. Do you think I care whether you call Me Yahweh, Jehovah, Allah, Wakantonka, Brahma, Father, Mother, or even the Void of Nirvana? Do you think I care which of My special children you feel closest to—Jesus, Mary, Buddha, Krishna, Mohammed, or any of the others? You can call Me and My Special Ones any name you choose, if only you would go about My business of loving one another as I love you. How can you keep neglecting something so simple?

I'm not telling you to abandon your religions. Enjoy your religions, honor them, learn from them, just as you should enjoy, honor, and learn from your parents. But do you walk around telling everyone that your parents are better than theirs? Your religion, like your parents, may always have the most special place in your heart; I don't mind that at all. And I don't want you to combine all the Great Traditions in One Big Mess. Each religion is unique for a reason. Each has a unique style so that people can find the best path for themselves.

But My Special Children—the ones that your religions revolve around—all live in the same place (My heart) and they get along perfectly, I assure you. The clergy must stop creating a myth of sibling rivalry where there is none.

My blessed children of Earth, the world has grown too small for your pervasive religious bigotries and confusion. The whole planet is connected by air travel, satellite dishes, telephones, fax machines, rock concerts, diseases, and mutual needs and concerns. Get with the program! If you really want to help, then commit yourselves to figuring out how to feed your hungry, clothe your naked, protect your abused, and shelter your poor.

And just as importantly, make your own everyday life a shining example of kindness and good humor. I've given you all the resources you need, if only you abandon your fear of each other and begin living, loving, and laughing together.

Finally, My Children everywhere, think of the life of Jesus and the fearlessness with which He chose to live and die. As I love Him, so do I love each one of you. I'm not really ticked off, I just want to grab your attention because I hate to see you suffer.

But I gave you free will. I just want you to be happy.

Always. Trust in Me.

Your One and Only,

God

> "Letter from God" by Bo Lozoff. First appeared in *Just Another Spiritual Book*, by Bo Lozoff, 1990. Human Kindness Foundation, PO Box 61619, Durham, NC 27715. Reprinted by permission.

What Did Jesus Really Say?

Did Jesus really say the Lord's Prayer and deliver the Sermon on the Mount as recorded in the New Testament? Probably not, according to a group of Bible experts who recently completed a six-year study of the sayings of Jesus. In fact, claim the scholars, more than 80 percent of the words ascribed to Jesus in the Gospels may be apocryphal. That includes Jesus's Eucharistic speech at the Last Supper ("Take, eat. This is my body…") and every word he is said to have uttered from the cross.

These are among the assertions of the Jesus Seminar, a controversial panel of about 50 liberal-to-moderate scholars from universities and divinity schools around the world who have embarked on a modern-day quest for the "historical Jesus." Applying some conventional methods of textual analysis and other more contentious rules of evidence, the scholars purport to identify the characteristics of Jesus's speech and to rule out "hearsay." Besides his reliance on short witticisms and parables, for example, Jesus often said the unexpected and unconventional, according to the scholars.

Based on their historical analysis, they have just published a much abridged "Gospel of Mark, Red Letter Edition," which argues that only 17 of 111 sayings attributed to Jesus in Mark's Gospel are authentic. In the book, published by Polebridge Press in Sonoma, Calif., the scholars have printed in red the words they are most confident Jesus spoke; those they believe he probably spoke are in pink; words he probably did not say but might reflect his thinking are in gray, and words they believe he could not have spoken are in black. There is one red verse in the entire book: "Pay to the emperor whatever belongs to the emperor and to God whatever belongs to God" (Mark 12:17).

Much of the rest, argues Robert Funk, head of the seminar's Westar Institute, consists of later additions to the oral tradition and reflects the thinking of church leaders decades after Jesus's death. "If I were a leader of this fledgling community of Christians and wanted my views remembered," says Funk, "I'd attribute them to Jesus."

That there are so few authentic sayings in the Gospels should not come as a surprise, says Funk. Only short, pithy aphorisms and a few memorable parables spoken by Jesus are likely to have survived the decades before the Gospels were written down, he contends. Passages considered likely to be authentic by the seminar include Jesus's paradoxical saying that "It is easier for a camel to go through the eye of a needle than for a rich man to enter into the kingdom of God."

As might be expected, Funk and his colleagues have plenty of detractors. Bible scholars from across the theological spectrum have challenged the seminar's methods and presumptions. Some see the project as a blatant attempt by theological liberals to discredit the Bible. The seminar's work, says Don A.

Carson, professor of New Testament at Trinity Evangelical Divinity School in Deerfield, Ill., is flawed by "left wing" ideology that is predisposed to reject anything supernatural. To argue that Jesus only spoke in aphorisms and parables, "is profoundly circular." And to rule out passages that reflect church traditions "assumes that the church didn't learn anything from Jesus." Howard Clark Kee, a New Testament professor emeritus at Boston University, has called the seminar's tactics "an academic disgrace." Its members, Kee wrote in a letter to the *Los Angeles Times*, seem determined to find a Jesus "free of such features, embarrassing to modern intellectuals, as demons, miracles, and predictions about the future."

The book, says Funk, is intended mainly to provide a resource for further scholarly study into the historical Jesus. Similarly abbreviated and annotated versions of the Gospels according to Matthew, Luke, and John as well as the apocryphal Gospel of Thomas, are due out later this year. Eventually, they will be combined into "The Five Gospels: Red Letter Edition," which Funk hopes will find its way into church pews and the hands of lay-people. "It should be helpful," he says, "to anyone who is looking for a different approach to biblical material, based on hard historical evidence."

The next phase of the seminar's study will be no less controversial. Starting in the fall, it will begin examining Jesus's miracles and deeds as recorded in the Gospels, including the Resurrection.

> by Jeffery L. Sheler © July 1, 1991, *U.S. News and World Report*.

Jesus Christ, Plain and Simple 7.1

"Who do you say that I am?"

When Jesus posed this question to his disciples in Matthew's Gospel, Peter emphatically and faithfully replied, "You are the Christ, the Son of the living God." And what might the answer be today? Three newly published scholarly books put forward a startlingly revisionist reply. While Jesus may have been a carpenter, that probably meant he was illiterate and belonged to a low caste of artisans. He did not preach salvation from sin through sacrifice; he never said "Blessed are the peacemakers for they shall be called sons of God"; neither did he say "Blessed are the pure in heart for they shall see God." For that matter, he probably never delivered the Sermon on the Mount. As for the question posed to Peter and the disciples, Jesus never asked it. And he never cured any diseases. As for the other miracles? No loaves and fishes, no water into wine, no raising of Lazarus. And certainly no resurrection. What happened to his body then? Most likely it was consumed by wild dogs.

Until now, this sort of *Bah, humbug!* approach to the Scriptures was in full display largely in the rarified and theologically correct atmosphere of seminaries and elite universities. John Dominic Crossan, a Bible scholar at DePaul University, notes that there was an "implicit deal—you scholars can go off to the universities and write in the journals and say anything you want." Now, he says, "the scholars are coming out of the closet," demanding public attention for the way they think. Among the latest such works are Crossan's *Jesus: A Revolutionary Biography* (Harper San Francisco; $18), Burton Mack's *The Lost Gospel* (Harper San Francisco; $22), and *The Five Gospels* (Macmillan; $30).

For Crossan, Jesus' deification was akin to the worship of Augustus Caesar—a mixture of myth, propaganda, and social convention. It was simply a thing that was done in the ancient Mediterranean world. Christ's pedigree—his virgin birth in Bethlehem of Judea, home of his reputed ancestor King David—is retrospective mythmaking by writers who had "already decided on the transcendental importance of the adult Jesus," Crossan says. The journey to Bethlehem from Nazareth, he adds, is "pure fiction, a creation of Luke's own imagination." He speculates that Jesus may not even have been Mary's firstborn and that the man the Bible calls his brother James was the eldest child. Crossan argues that Jesus did not cure anyone but that he did "heal" people by refusing to ostracize them because of their illnesses.

While Jesus may have had some ability to use trancelike therapies to "exorcise" demons, Crossan says, he used the incidents themselves chiefly to characterize "Roman imperialism as demonic possession." Both Crossan and Mack say Jesus' ideas are similar to those of the Cynics of the age. These were men who believed not in nothing, as the word now implies, but in the rejection of the standard beliefs and values of society. And so, contrary to the times, Jesus taught radical egalitarianism. He also demanded itinerancy of his disciples. Believing that such wanderlust subtly spread subversion, the Romans had him crucified. Jesus—a peasant nobody—was never buried, never taken by his friends to a rich man's sepulcher. Rather, says Crossan, the tales of entombment and resurrection were latter-day wishful thinking. Instead, Jesus' corpse went the way of all abandoned criminals' bodies: it was probably barely covered with dirt, vulnerable to the wild dogs that roamed the wasteland of the execution grounds.

Mack agrees with most of Crossan's reconception of Jesus' life. But the main purpose of *The Lost Gospel* is to propagate *The Book of Q*, a back-to-basics teaching of the original Christians that was teased out of ancient texts by scholars who believe that it predates the Gospels. (Q stands for the German *Quelle*, which means "source.") *The Book of Q* has no narrative. Rather it is a collection of sayings and aphorisms. Mack says the "Jesus people" were attracted to his teachings because he preached the holiness of the simple life. Thus verses like "Turn the other cheek," "Love your enemies," and "Rejoice when reproached," all part of *Q*, embody the practices of a community of charity, hope, and neighborliness. Mack writes, "The narrative Gospels have no claim as historical accounts. The Gospels are imaginative creations."

If Jesus amounts to only his words in *The Lost Gospel*, he barely holds on to them in *The Five Gospels.* The book is the product of the 74 biblical scholars (including Crossan) who belong to the Jesus Seminar. Meeting twice a year, the group votes with purposeful theatricality on the authenticity of each Gospel saying, casting color-coded beads into a box to indicate which lines of Christ were holier than others. The latest round appears in *The Five Gospels*, which, parodying the red-letter Bibles that display the words of Jesus in red type, prints the supposedly authentic words in red and prints the rest, in descending order of credibility, in other colors. The text is a breezy new colloquial translation. Precisely 82% of Jesus' words are judged inauthentic.

And what is the fifth gospel? It is the Gospel of Thomas, which church fathers deemed unacceptable because it contained ideas of the heretical Gnostic sects. Indeed, the book ends with Jesus rebuking Peter for trying to oust a woman named Mary from the company of disciples. "Females are not worthy of life," says Peter. Jesus replies, "Look, I shall guide her to make her a male, so that she too may become a living spirit resembling you males. For every female who makes herself male will enter heaven's kingdom." Three sentences in Thomas survive the seminar's judgment as likely statements of Jesus'. (The members of the seminar voted down the Mary passage.)

Not surprisingly, the new books are controversial. Jacob Neusner, professor of religious studies at the University of South Florida, calls the Jesus Seminar "either the greatest scholarly hoax since the Piltdown Man or the utter bankruptcy of New Testament studies—I hope the former." Other scholars question the use of the Thomas and the hypothetical Q. The effect is like looking through the wrong end of a telescope at a vanishing Jesus. In his forthcoming *The Gospel of Jesus* (Westminster), William R. Farmer, professor emeritus of the New Testament at Southern Methodist University, decries the latest Q theory because it leads to the bizarre conclusion that "the death and resurrection of Jesus was . . . of little or no importance to his disciples." Meanwhile, N. T. Wright, an Oxford University teacher and newly named cathedral dean in Lichfield, England, says it is a "freshman mistake" to suppose that the Gospels do not refer to actual events simply because the writers of Matthew, Mark, Luke, and John have clear points of view. One of the most formidable of traditionalist Bible scholars, Wright, whose conservative rejoinder *Jesus and the Victory of God* (Fortress) is forthcoming, says the skeptical theories also fail to provide any credible explanation for how a faith founded by their pared-down Jesus could spread so rapidly after his crucifixion. Wright's explanation: the resurrection.

As Wright sees it, playing the game of deconstructing the New Testament nowadays "is like finding yourself in the middle of a rugby field with five teams and 10 balls. There is all kinds of excitement: everybody is tackling everybody, and everyone thinks he's on the winning team." For the moment, it is impossible for ordinary churchgoers to follow the action, much less determine which of the competing Jesuses will win.

> by Richard N. Ostling © 1994, *Time*, Inc. Reprinted by permission.

Broken Bodies

Lesson

12.2

(Mark 5:7–8; Mark 10:33–34)

"Did you ever capture enemies?"

They hesitated. What in the world was I getting at? Why would I want to bring up the past like that?

Of the twelve men in the Bible house, some were of the older vintage. Some were known as "fight chiefs" in their day. Owarape Ali was there, and Eleké Whi Ali, men still distinguished as "big men" around the village.

Some in the room had listened to the Talk. A few hadn't—but even they were struck by the qualities of the Man Jesus, His character, His teaching, and His acts.

By the time we reached the fifth chapter, Jesus had gathered disciples, healed the sick, calmed the storm, and generally let His identity be known. Even the spirits gave testimony to who He was.

The Folopa loved the boldness with which Jesus approached the wild man in the Gerasene tombs. That man was a beast. No man could subdue him and chains could not hold him; night and day he would cry out and cut himself with stones. But the real source of his strength, not to mention his agony, was manifest when he ran up to Jesus, fell at His feet, and shouted at the top of his voice:

"What do you want with me, Jesus, Son of the Most High God? Swear to God that you won't torture me!" For Jesus was saying to him, "Come out of this man, you evil spirit!" (Mark 5:7–8).

We got to the middle of that verse and could go no further; we did not have a word for "torture." That's when I asked them if they had ever captured enemies.

They said they had.

I groped further. "When you captured them, did you ever hit them with sticks or anything like that?"

By this time their eyes were boring holes through me.

Finally Hapele caught on to what I was getting at and ventured a few descriptions.

Soon others, especially the older ones, joined in with a cascade of graphic descriptions of the worst torture I'd ever heard…like the times they would hold torches up to the captured person's skin until it blistered, or they'd pour boiling water on him until the skin literally came off. Or they'd tie him spread-eagled and naked to the ground and have the women beat him with their digging sticks, concentrating particularly on the private parts.

Or they would tie the enemy to a stake and with a bamboo knife, cut off a bicep, take it to the fire, cook it, and return to stand in front of him, taking bites saying, "I'm eating your flesh."

Now it was my eyes which bored holes through them.

It was obviously far better to die outright at the hands of these warriors than to be captured, taken back to the village and killed slowly. With the constant revenge killings, there was an abject hatred for the group that had last raided and killed members of their village. Nothing was bad enough.

I was stunned. Who am I working with? I thought. All I had done was to explore around a little to find a word and it was like I had turned the key to open the bottomless pit. No wonder they'd reacted as they had when I asked my question. In any case, yes, they did have a word for torture, *susupu eratapó*. And if the demons in Mark 5 had had anything like this in mind—though it was the very stuff they had been instigating in the world down through time—it was no wonder they were afraid.

About a week later we broached the subject again. We'd moved up to Mark 10. This time it wasn't demons fearing torment; rather it was Jesus predicting what was about to happen to Him.

"We are going up to Jerusalem," he said, "and the Son of Man will be betrayed to the chief priests and teachers of the law. They will condemn him to death and will hand him over to the Gentiles, who will mock him and spit on him, flog him and kill him. Three days later he will rise" (Mark 10:33–34).

Again we were stuck. I didn't have a word for "flog."

"What do you call it," I asked, "if someone hits another, say an enemy, with something like a rope?"

That drew a blank. Apparently hitting someone with a rope was nothing that sounded familiar to them. But it was about to happen to Jesus and it was part of the passage so I cast about for other ways to describe it. My eyes fell on a piece of rattan vine left over from tying the thatch on the roof. It was lying on the old wood-stove. The vine was about three feet long and as thick as my little finger. I went around the table, picked it up, and instructed the men to imagine the vine was a piece of rope and the woodstove was the back of Jesus. Then with all my might I started beating the iron top of the stove.

Immediately Owarape Ali—his eyes wild and his nostrils flaring—shouted out: "That's not hitting with a rope, that's *fokosó sirapó*!" He was indignant, staring up at me from his place on the floor.

Fokosó sirapó. I walked back around the table and wrote the words down.

"Tell me more about it," I said.

But when I looked up they were all just staring at me. It was like it had taken them right back to the old days.

"Wait a minute," someone said. "Do you mean to say they did THAT to Jesus?"

"Yes."

"But here He just said they were going to do it. Did they really do it to Him?"

"Yes."

Quiet fell on the room. Finally Eleké Whi Ai said, "We used to do that. But we only did it to our enemies, and then just before we were going to kill them."

"Yes," I said, "that is coming, too."

Heads were down. In the corners, the large shell earrings of the old men swung back and forth in utter dejection. The memory of *fokosó sirapó* 'floggings' was too fresh in their minds. They were seeing a deeper vision of the abject cruelty—the enormity of it all—than I had ever considered. And that this would happen to Jesus…someone they had grown to respect and like. He was a Man who would put little children on His lap, who would reach out and heal those in need, a man who could hardly have an enemy. These men knew what torturing and flogging were all about. That this Jesus would come to suffer like this was just too much to take in.

We had to stop for the morning.

Payback

(Luke 22:19–20)

When we first started living in Fukutao, it was only God's grace that protected me from my ignorance. That hasn't changed, but over the years we've learned a few things.

It was very early in our first term when I learned firsthand about payback. We didn't know a lot of what was going on around us yet. We'd done our homework and reading, of course, as part or our orientation. But it's not the same as finding things out by living them.

We were building our house and I was up on the roof. We hadn't put the thatch on yet and I was in the process of cutting one of the rafters that was sticking up too high. People were all around, some watching, some helping, and I called out for someone to hand me an ax. A man from another village, Wei Ali, picked up an ax and handed it to me. As I pulled it up, it caught on something and jerked on my hand. The ax slid away and went over the edge, falling on and grazing Wei Ali. The skin cut was only slight, thank God, but it had put a good tear in his shirt.

Immediately there was a great commotion. People were yelling and shouting, looking at Wei Ali and looking back at me. It was apparent that a terrible thing had just happened and I had done it.

I came off the roof as fast as I could to check him over. There was a little blood, but it wasn't bad. With genuine concern I got my first-aid kit out, put some antiseptic ointment on the cut, and bandaged it up. It would heal and everybody knew it; these people had seen a good deal more than this.

But the incident wasn't closed. Everyone was waiting. Tense. Troubled. Expectant.

People continued what seemed like bickering back and forth, all in high-volumed excitement. I couldn't understand enough language to make sense of it, and I didn't know what else to do.

Wei Ali was still agitated, standing there with his new bandage and his torn shirt. I looked at that shirt. It had never been any great piece of fabric, and it looked like it had seen long service of almost daily wear. But now it was not simply old, it was torn.

Maybe if I paid for it, I thought, that might make him feel better. With all eyes following my every move, I went over to my bags, fished out a couple of *kinas* 'dollars' and gave them to him.

As soon as I did that, in full sight of everyone as it was, everything changed. He smiled broadly and everybody quieted down. Justice had apparently been covered. I had done the right thing. Everything was even again and we were all back to normal.

As far as I was concerned, I had only showed appropriate concern. The wound needed dressing; I dressed it. The shirt needed replacing; I gave him some money. But to them it went far deeper that that.

Accidents don't just happen around here, or at least they aren't passed off as easily as that. For every act of harm, whether intentional or accidental, there always has to be some sort of compensation to even out the score.

All this was my first encounter with payback, the most basic of underlying structures in traditional Melanesian societies. In the past it was always the basis for tribal warfare—the continuous cycle of vendetta killings. These have always been "eye for eye, tooth for tooth" societies. When I inflicted injury, I had not only done damage, but caused a loss of face as well, and I had to pay. The money wasn't so much to replace the shirt as to make things right. It was a matter of moral restitution.

With such a system in place, it's easy for people to see how restitution is necessary when God has been offended. One man may sin against another, but ultimately the sin is against God. He is the One who has said do not lie, do not steal, do not commit adultery. When we break those laws something has to be done, not just in compensation to the person offended but to God Himself.

The fact that we're powerless to do this and that God took the initiative and sent His Son to do it for us, is what the gospel is all about. The Folopa know this, at least those who have listened to the Talk do. The death of Jesus is the payback for our offenses. He paid the price that was too heavy for anyone else. That Jesus suffered and died—willingly and terribly—is very meaningful to the Folopa. Somehow they are more tender toward that truth than we are. It doesn't take much to send them into a deep silence of contemplation.

It was years after that first encounter with payback when we translated Luke 22. It wasn't an easy passage to handle. Jesus was with His disciples, observing the tradition of Passover for the last time. All the symbolism of the slain

Passover lamb would shortly be fulfilled in His own death. He would become the appeasement before God for the sins of men.

With the completion of these old symbols, however, He introduced new ones to serve as reminders. The bread would stand for the breaking of His body and the wine for His spilled blood.

> And he took bread, gave thanks and broke it, and gave it to them, saying, "This is my body given for you. Do this in remembrance of me." In the same way, after the supper he took the cup, saying, "This cup is the new covenant in my blood, which is poured out for you" (Luke 22:19–20).

We had some difficulty with the word for body. Because of customary usage that had preceded us, they wanted to translate it *mi* or "meat." That's how the pastor who came here talked about it, they said.

Communion services among the Folopa are very solemn. Without any grapes or bread in the area they use sweet potato and lemon juice instead. It's all they have, and it is enough.

In translating, they explained to me how the lemon juice stands for blood and the sweet potato stands for meat. It made sense to them since they saw meat and blood as parallel terms.

I saw their point but had to disagree. That was not what the Bible was saying. The Bible is talking about body, not meat, and the word for body is *tiki*.

We discussed this for some time. I saw how easy it would be to employ the term "meat" and think it was perfectly right. Especially here. Papua New Guineans have had a history of eating meat—and human meat at that. It would be a natural tie-in…but that was not the meaning Jesus intended when He said, "This is my body."

It was in His body that He ministered on earth, that He took the abuse, that He died. It was an act of His whole personality—mind, will, feelings, and spirit. His whole being suffered the penalty for our sins.

He took our punishment. On Himself. In His body.

As for "blood," that was pretty straightforward. Blood is blood. In the Bible blood is a symbol for life. It also has everything to do with the most solemn of covenants.

We translated "covenant" with the term for "binding agreement." But it was not easy to show how the blood was what made the binding agreement stick.

Jesus' saying, "This cup is the new covenant in my blood," was difficult to translate because the idea of blood having anything to do with a binding agreement was puzzling. How could an agreement be "in my blood"? Making it harder, the Folopa do not have any direct translation for "in." I looked at another version of the Bible in English and found the wording, "This is the blood of the covenants." That didn't help either!

Our Lord's original hearers had no problem with this—at least not with the language. "The blood of the covenant" was something clear in their culture and history.

But how to say it in Folopa?

It took us some time to get it. The fact that the Folopa had been observing communion for years without fully understanding it didn't help us. Finally we settled on using the word, *eratapó,* 'to bring into being'. It would serve as the missing connector between blood and covenant. It was the blood that brought the covenant into being. It ratified the agreement. It made it happen.

The Folopa think about these things a great deal: that Jesus really lived, suffered, and died for them. And they think about it most when they observe communion—even though what it was all about had never been a complete connection. But now it was made clear—the blood was not just symbolizing a life put to death but was symbolic of God's agreement.

Agreements are usually between two people—here it would be between man and God. But as man is fallible and could not keep his side of it, God had to make the covenant with Himself, through His own Son.

Now, bound in the blood of God's Son, the agreement is permanent. The significance began to come through to the Folopa. In communion, we're not just remembering the actual, physical death of Jesus on the cross but observing again the agreement that God made with His Son for our sakes.

The payback has been paid in full. It is a revolutionary truth in any society—but particularly so where payback is everything.

It's *beté* at the deepest level.

Ransom

(Mark 10:45)

Jesus died, but not for nothing.

He died as a ransom for many. He told about it on several occasions before it happened. He wove it into His teachings on how His followers are to live, which is almost always the opposite of what our natural sense would tell us. Such came out in the passage we were working on in Mark:

> "Whoever wants to become great among you must be your servant, and whoever wants to be first must be slave of all. For even the Son of Man did not come to be served, but to serve, and to give his life as a ransom for many" (Mark 10:43–45).

Ransom, ransom, I thought, what is the word for ransom? This is the heart of the gospel—the *beté* of the whole message.

The men around the table had that common blank expression on their faces that must have reflected my own. Here we go again, they seemed to be thinking. He's looking for a word. What is it?

It was often like this. A game of twenty questions.

"I'm thinking of something and you've got to tell me what it is."

"Do we get any hints?"

"I'll try," I said. "Back to the fighting days. You took captives, right?"

"Yes."

"Were there ever times when you offered to release the person alive—say, to trade the man or woman or child for whatever you could get, like shells or pigs or anything like that?"

The question was absurd to them. Their laughter sent hints of ridicule and I hesitated to probe again. To have ever considered something so materialistic was beneath them. Their wars and killings had always been to avenge death. It was just to keep the score even—period.

Hapele, however, was thinking and seemed to grasp what I was getting at. "We do have something like that," he said. "It's not quite the same. It was never used with an enemy, but we do use it between clans. It's *duputapó*."

I knew the word. It means "trade."

"Tell me about it," I said.

"You know," he said. "Things have to always be kept even. But sometimes you can't keep them even, not perfectly, when your own people are involved. It's like what happened with Wótale," he said.

"What happened with Wótale?" I asked.

"Well," he continued, "not long ago we were making a new garden and Wótale was cutting one of the big trees. Just down the hill from him a woman was working sago. They knew of each other's presence and Wótale kept warning her to move, but she wanted to get a little more done first. She knew it was going to take a while to get that big tree down, so she kept working.

"When Wótale finished the undercut he yelled to her again but she still didn't leave. Then suddenly—and earlier than either of them expected—the tree groaned and began to fall. He yelled and she ran, but there was no way to get clear. The tree fell right on her, crushed her skull and she died.

"What followed was a terrible uproar. Wótale got out of there as fast as he could, hiding himself in his men's house and all the clansmen of the dead woman immediately went for their bows and arrows and axes. As one body they marched up to Wótale's longhouse and stood outside yelling and shouting and demanding justice. They were calling for Wótale's life for the life of the woman he'd killed."

"'But it was an accident,'" his clan brothers protested from inside the longhouse.

"'It doesn't matter. He did it,' they all shouted back."

"'But he warned her!' they yelled out."

"'That's no matter!' they yelled back."

"Wótale never came out, but after a while his clan brothers did, and they brought things with them. They began spreading objects out on the ground, starting with pieces of bark cloth, *kina* 'abalone' shells, red cloth, axes, bush knives, salt. They were all valuables, things they would never give up except under great duress. They also drove stakes in the ground and tethered pigs to them.

"As the stock of goods kept growing, the woman's clan didn't subside in their yelling threats, and Wótale's people were doing a lot of yelling back. It was all bargaining and bickering for how much it would take to pay for a life. It went on and on at high pitch until somebody from the woman's clan yelled, 'Supó.'"

Supó means "enough!"

"Then the leader of the men's house said, '*Duputapó*.'

"That completed it. There was a trade. The bereaved clan picked up all the valuables, leading the pigs on their tethers, and went home. Then Wótale came out into the open and was free to resume normal life without fear of further reprisal."

"How would it be if we used that word in this verse?" I said. I wrote out something rough: "We were in jeopardy of being killed but Jesus came to make a trade. He gave His life up instead and we got to go free."

"*Duputapó*." Hapele nodded. "And God said, '*Supó*.'"

"That's right."

One of the old men had been listening intently. He leaned forward, a big *kina* shell swinging on his bare chest.

"That's hard to believe," he said.

"What is?" I said.

"That *duputapó* was a person. In the past we've given a great deal to trade for a clan brother. A great deal. But we've never given a person. And a person would never give himself!"

He looked around at the others, the whites of his eyes flaring in deep-set sockets. He leaned back with a sigh, like it was beyond his grasp. Then he said what they always say when things hit them at the deepest level: "We are dying of the deliciousness of this talk."

> by Neil Anderson and Hyatt Moore. Chapter 16, "Broken Bodies"; Chapter 18, "Payback"; Chapter 19, "Ransom." Reprinted from *In Search of the Source: A First Encounter with God's Word,* with permission from Wycliffe Bible Translators, USA.

Unbiblical Blackjack

14.2

Lesson

The scriptural trump card: Proper biblical interpretation allows no contradiction

I was listening to my car radio the other day to a local talk show. I forget what the subject was, but some lady called in and quoted a verse of Scripture to prove or illustrate her point. She was way off the mark, but that is not the subject of this story. The radio host responded something like this: "Are we just going to quote verses to each other? My verse tops your verse?" In this way, he simply disposed of Scripture, refusing even to consider it in the conversation. This same tack was taken by a feminist in a Christian college recently when students tried to confront her with passages from the Apostle Paul. Is this the latest fad in avoiding the Word of God?

This approach shows a weak view of Scripture, at the least, and outright rebellion at the worst. Jesus quoted the Scriptures constantly in His ministry, and so did the apostles in their writings. If someone used a passage wrongly, our Lord didn't just "trump" their verse with another one, but showed how their interpretation was wrong. (See John 8:33–38 for one example.)

Scripture does not contradict itself, so scriptural discussions do not involve piling up contradictory Scriptures until one side prevails against the other.

Rebellion is consistent in trying to find some place to hide from God. It seeks to cover itself from the blinding light of God's Word, to shift responsibility away, to appear to love righteousness and truth. Even Satan's ministers come disguised as ministers of righteousness (2 Corinthians 11:15). What better way than to neutralize the Scriptures?

It is true that many Christians today have not been taught that the Bible sets forth a system of Christian truth. Their knowledge of the Bible is truncated, episodic, and fragmented. Too often their discussions involve simply throwing Scripture at each other without understanding that every interpretation of Scripture involves a framework of thought. There is no attempt to understand each other's framework, or to see how each verse fits into the framework of God's revelation of himself. Such discussions too often bear the semblance of a religious game of high-card.

Many modern Christians respond the same way when confronted with the clear teachings of Scripture. If they can find some passage or verse that seems to contradict the given passage, they smugly lay aside the Bible and continue to think their own thoughts.

There is a better way. The Bible is the revelation of God himself to his people. The end of Scripture is that we might know God. All the truth of the Bible, then, is to this end: the glory and knowledge of God. I must labor to submit my thoughts and my ways to God (Isaiah 55:7, 8).

This means that God has thoughts and ways. They are not like ours, and we can never attain to them, but we are called to thoughts and ways that are the image of his thoughts and ways. This we can do.

David prayed, "Remove from me the way of lying: and grant me thy law graciously. I have chosen the way of truth: thy judgments I have laid before me" (Psalm 119:29, 30).

Once Christians abandon the mutual consideration of Scripture, they fall into an evil far worse than the game of Scripture high-card. They simply try to trump each other's ideas with their own ideas. The church becomes even more fragmented and splintered, to the shame of the church and the delight of the devil.

So, quote your Scripture to me, please. I will not try to refute you with another Scripture, but I will attempt to understand how your Scripture fits into the general sense of Scripture and how it reveals the glory and majesty of God. If I am right in my understanding, each Scripture will complement, not contradict, other passages of Scripture. I am never called to believe one part of Scripture at the expense of some other part.

> by C. W. Powell Reprinted by permission from *World* magazine, Asheville, NC. (800) 951-6397.

Remade in Our Image

How we interpret our most sacred text will have a profound impact on the respect we show, or refuse to show, to lesser texts. And in American history, we see the church's disrespect for the text of Scripture followed, imitatively, by disrespect in our culture at large for lesser documents. As Christians, we are the people of the Word, and how we treat the Word will affect how we and others respect the meaning of words.

This explains how we have come to handle the Constitution of the United States the way we do. The prevailing sentiment in our courts today is that the Constitution is a "living document" and that we should not attempt to tie it down to the "original intent" of the framers. But if we are not to be bound by the intent of the framers, why not dispense with the framers entirely, and with the very idea of a written constitution? If all we wanted was a blank screen on which to project our current desires, then it would seem that all those curious, old-fashioned words just get in the way.

The reason we do this is that we want to have it both ways. Suppose we had judges who delivered their skewed rulings and, when pressed, said that they did this because it seemed like a good idea at the time. They had too much pizza the night before, and the ruling came to them in a dream. The general public would be upset, and the game would be over. But, in contrast, if they limited themselves to the plain meaning of the Constitution, their experiment in political engineering would be over. And so the Constitution must be kept around to provide the smell of a hoary antiquity, while a relativistic hermeneutic is slapped on to provide judges with the untrammeled liberty of doing whatever they want.

Jesus taught us to pray, asking the Father to treat us just the same way that we treat our enemies. During the past century or so, the Christian church in our nation has mishandled the Bible in remarkable ways, and has reinterpreted her own creeds and confessions in a fashion that can only be described as entirely dishonest. By this we were asking God to give us civil rulers who would behave in exactly the same way with our civil texts. We now see He has granted our request—and sent leanness to our souls.

> by Douglas Wilson. Reprinted from *Tabletalk* magazine, February 1999, 60–61. Used with permission of Ligonier Ministries, PO Box 547500, Orlando, FL 32854; (800) 435-4343.

Enuma Elish

The *Enuma Elish*—probably the most famous of the ancient Near Eastern texts—is the main source of information concerning Babylonian cosmology [a branch of philosophy that deals with the origin of the world or universe]. The epic poem was not written primarily as an account of origins, however. Rather, its purposes were to praise Marduk, the main god of Babylon; to explain his rise from a great but local deity to the head of the whole pantheon [all the gods of a people]; and to honor Babylon itself as the most preeminent city. The account of creation is used as a background to the real story of divine struggles and the establishment of Marduk's supremacy.

The Epic of Creation, as it is often called, derived its proper name from the first words of its opening line: *"Enuma elish la nabu shamanu. . . ."*—literally, "When above the heaven had not [yet] been named. . . ." It begins with Apsu (the ocean) and Tiamat (the primeval waters) lying inert together and eventually producing the divine natural forces: Lahmu and Lahamu (silt and slime), Anshar and Kishar (the horizons of sky and earth), Anu (heaven, the principle of authority), and Nudimmud (or Ea, waters of the earth, the principle of wisdom). As the offspring grew, they began to order the chaotic world and become rebellious. Apsu and Tiamat, resentful and angry, tried to reassert themselves. They called on Mummu (mist of the clouds, the principle of entropy) and together conspired to slay the young gods they had begotten. The plan failed, however, as Tiamat withdrew out of motherly concern and the wise Ea (earth water) slew Apsu (ocean) with his art and cunning (as presumably the waters were contained for purposes of irrigation in the first stage of Mesopotamian civilization) and locked Mummu (mist, entropy) away. Later, with his wife Damkina, Ea produced his magnificent son Marduk.

From there, the myth charts Marduk's dramatic rise to power. When Tiamat created monsters and married their chief Kingu in an effort to slay the young gods, Marduk was summoned to control her. In return for his efforts, he demanded and received recognition from the gods as the supreme one. Enthroned and feted, Marduk went forth, slew Tiamat, and then ordered the chaos by fixing the places of the stars, establishing the roles of the gods, separating heaven and earth, and, finally, setting up Babylon as his dwelling place. Almost as an afterthought, the rebellious Kingu was killed, and from his blood the wise Ea made mankind to do the bidding of the gods. The myth ends with elaborate praises of Marduk and a recitation of his fifty names.

Although the *Enuma Elish* was discovered in the ruins of King Ashurbanipol's (668–626 B.C.) library at Nineva, it probably dates from a much earlier time when Babylon rose to political supremacy and its deity Marduk became a national god. These events took place during the First Babylonian Dynasty (2057–1758 B.C.) and most particularly in the reign of the powerful King Hammurabi (c. 1900 B.C.). But much of the material is even older than that, dating back to the Babylonians' predecessors in the region, the Sumerians. Many of the names in the *Enuma Elish* are Sumerian, and some, such as

Apsu, Anu, and Enlil, are Sumerian gods. While a great deal of Babylonian mythology seems derivative of the Sumerians', it is impossible to be exact about the *Enuma Elish,* because no Sumerian prototype has been discovered.

The *Enuma Elish* was written for recitation and was enacted annually on the fourth day of the New Year's festival before a statue of Marduk. In ritually performing the myth, not only was the cosmos symbolically recreated but the order of the world was reconfirmed. The king knelt before the high priest of Marduk and submitted himself (and the state he represented) to humiliation before the god and his power. Rededicating himself in this fashion, the world was reestablished, the divine lease renewed, and the connection between the absolute and the relative, the eternal and the temporal, restored.

> *Enuma Elish.* Excerpted from pages 91–92 of *Primal Myths* by Barbara C. Sproul. © 1979 by Barbara C. Sproul. Reprinted by permission of HarperCollins Publishers, Inc.

Glossary

Glossary

absolute> Having no restriction, exception, or qualification; fundamental, ultimate; **absolutes>** Immutable rules or principles; direct commands from the transcendent, personal Creator to humans.

agnostic> A person who holds the view that God is unknown and probably unknowable; one who is not yet committed to believing in either the existence or nonexistence of God; **agnosticism>** The view of an agnostic.

animism> Belief that all natural objects and phenomena (such as trees, stones, the wind) have souls; belief that truth comes through a witch doctor, shaman, or spirit guide, who interprets dreams and visions to explain what the spirits think and what they want people to do.

anthropomorphism> An interpretation of what is not human or personal in terms of human or personal characteristics; God is often described with human characteristics.

apocrypha> Books included in the Septuagint and Vulgate but excluded from the Jewish and Protestant canons of the Old Testament; **apocryphal>** of doubtful authenticity.

apologetic> A reasoned defense; **apologetics>** A branch of theology devoted to the defense of belief in the personal, eternal Creator and His Word.

atheism> The doctrine that God does not exist.

authentic> Conforming to an original; genuine, having been made, done, or written, by the person who is claimed to have done it; worthy of acceptance or belief as conforming to or based on fact.

authority> A person or group holding the ability, power, or right to control and command.

autograph> An author's original manuscript.

bibliology> The study of the Bible and how it came to us.

canon> An authoritative list of books accepted as Holy Scripture.

catechize> To give religious instruction systematically, especially by questions, answers, and explanations and corrections.

condescend> To waive the privileges of rank; **condescension >** The act of stooping to the 'level' of another.

conviction> A strong persuasion or belief. [Presuppositions support absolutes, general principles, and convictions, in that order. A conviction is not a doctrine but an individual approach to daily issues over which other Christians may disagree: e.g., participating in theater, watching television, or drinking wine with dinner.]

culture> The customary beliefs, social forms, and material traits of a national, religious, or social group; **cultural >** Of or relating to a particular culture.

deconstructionism> A method of literary criticism that assumes language has its own meaning depending upon the reader or listener, and regardless of the author's intention.

demagoguery> Making use of popular prejudices and false claims and promises in order to gain power.

doctrine> A belief about a theological issue. [From a word meaning "teaches" or "instructs."]

ethics> The principles of conduct governing an individual or a group. [Answers the question, *What should I do?* and differs from values, which answer the question, *What is acceptable?*]

etymology > The history of a word shown by tracing its development since its earliest recorded occurrence in the language.

exegetical > Derived out of a statement or text; allowing the passage to speak for itself.

fact > An actual, objective, verifiable person, place, event, or thing.

faith > Belief or worldview. [Faith has content (what is believed), is credible (what is verifiable), and necessitates commitment (personal action based on facts).]

heresy > A doctrine or practice contrary to the truth of Scripture; **heretic** > A dissenter from established doctrine.

hermeneutics > The study of the interpretation of the Bible.

historicity > Historical actuality. [Answers the question, *Did something happen to a real person in real space and time?*]

humanism > The belief that humans are the beginning and end of all things and that human reason is sufficient to discover truth apart from divine revelation.

ideal > Based on absolute, immutable law. [In a sinful world, the ideal often conflicts with the real.]

illumination > Spiritual or intellectual enlightenment.

immanence > Closeness to, care for. [God's immanence is seen in His personal interest in His creation.]

immutable > Not capable of change. [Only God Himself is absolutely immutable.]

indoctrinate > To instruct in basic beliefs.

inspiration > The belief that all Scripture is God-breathed, every word and every part of every word.

interpret > To explain or tell the meaning of something, based on the author's original intention.

interpretation > An understanding and explanation of what a text meant to *them, then*—the people and time for which it was intended.

monotheism > The doctrine or belief that there is just one God.

multiculturalism > A belief that individuals and societies should accept, reflect, and adapt to diverse cultures.

mythology > Traditional, nonhistorical, and imaginary stories dealing with the gods and legendary heroes of a particular people.

naturalism > A belief that a person finds truth only in the external world through the five senses and the scientific method. [Ecclesiastes calls this "under the sun"; read: "what you see is what you get."]

nihilism > A belief that truth is dead; there is no meaning; nothing matters.

orthodox > Conforming to an established doctrine; based on an original source or authority.

pantheism > A belief that the personal experience of becoming one with the universe creates truth that cannot be measured or defined.

paraphrase > A restatement of a text, passage, or work in different words.

penultimate > Next to the last in a series.

polytheism > A belief in or worship of more than one god.

postmodernism> A belief that truth is relative to the culture or the group; that all reality, knowledge, experience, language, history, and ethics are created by those who hold them; and that all truth claims are to be tolerated.

preference> Something that is liked better than something else.

presupposition> Something that is assumed to be true.

providential> From God, who personally plans and oversees all things. [There is no such thing as accident, chance, destiny, fate, or luck because all these are impersonal.]

real> Having independent existence, whether visible or invisible; genuine.

relativism> A theory that knowledge is based on the limited nature of the mind and the conditions of knowing; a view that ethical truths depend on the individuals and groups holding them, that absolutes do not exist.

reliable> Consistent; stable.

revelation> An act of revealing or communicating divine truth. [God communicated truth to humans that was not known before.] **natural revelation**> Knowledge of God acquired from people, laws, events, times, and places, all of which bear marks of the Creator; **supernatural revelation**> The written Word (Scripture) and the living Word (Jesus) as they explain God to humans.

self-authentication> Proof that one is authentic and is therefore worthy of acceptance.

sovereign> Having unlimited power and independence, controlling everything that happens; **sovereignty**> The condition of having unlimited power and independence; God's rule over His creation.

subjective> Relating to an individual's feeling, opinion, or perspective on something.

theism> A belief that there is a God.

transcendent> Outside of and separate from the natural world.

translation> A rendering of a text into another language.

truth> That which conforms to reality; that which is actual, or in accordance with reality.

universal> Existing everywhere or under all conditions.

worldview> A philosophy, or set of beliefs, that begins with certain assumptions, or presuppositions, and answers the basic human questions concerning purpose, ethics, knowledge, God, and humanity.

Timeless Truth